A Widow's Tale

Mary Ethelyn Wightman

January 6, 2020

ISBN 978-1-0980-3815-1 (paperback)
ISBN 978-1-0980-3816-8 (digital)

Christian Faith Publishing, Inc.
832 Park Avenue
Meadville, PA 16335
www.christianfaithpublishing.com

Printed in the United States of America

Preface

Hi. My name is Penelope Bauer Wightisle. Almost everyone calls me Merr. You thought I was going to say Penny, didn't you?

When my first granddaughter, Chloe, was born, I used to go by her house, sing to her, and hold her. When she was a little less than a year old, every time I would go to her house, she would say, "Merrily, Merrily." I would then sing, "Row, row, row your boat, gently down the stream. Merrily, merrily, merrily, merrily. Life is but a dream."

One night, I finally realized that she thought that Merrily Merrily was my name. I had wanted to be called Gram because I thought that sounded upscale. But nothing can be better than being named by your own granddaughter, so the name Gram was a thing of the past. Through the years, my name became shortened to Merrily, and then Merr. But I'm getting ahead of myself.

My story is fiction, based on fact. Like the '50s television show, *Dragnet*: "The names have been changed to protect the innocent"— most of them anyway.

I was going to call my story, A Widow's Tail, because my whole life seems to have had an animal somewhere in it, but then I thought you might just think I couldn't spell or know the difference between the words *tail* and *tale*, so I'm going to call my story, *A Widow's Tale*.

Acknowledgments

Special Thanks to Claude, Ruthie, Ronnie, Mike, and Kendall.

They Met

My mom met my dad when he was driving one of those tour buses that had a luggage compartment underneath the bus. Dad had bright round hazel eyes, a trim body, and very little hair since he was twenty years old. Mom said that when Dad reached under the bus to get her luggage from the belly of the bus and came up with that mischievous grin of his, she was hooked. When he asked if she'd go out with him, she said yes, and the rest is history. She was in college at the University of Maryland, but she dropped out to marry him.

My grandmother was none too happy because not only did she drop out of school, but his family was from Germany. His oldest brother, Jack, was born in Germany. My grandmother did not appreciate some n'ere do well marrying her daughter. My grandmother loved my mom, but she had to show her displeasure in some way, so she purchased a silverware set for twelve people for their wedding gift and had it monogrammed with the letter T. Sounds okay until you realize that Grandmother was a Taylor, and Mom married a Bauer.

Florida

Frank was thirteen years old when I was born. He was lonely and happy to have a sister. He had a few friends, but he was quiet and stayed around Mom most of the time. He looked just like Dad, only with lots of black hair, and he was husky, but not fat. Frank loved Aunt Sophie because she had taught him how to play the piano, and he knew the two of them would play Chop Styx duets, and sing and do all the musical things music teachers knew how to do, just like they used to before he moved to Florida.

Mom's older sister, Aunt Sophie, and her husband, Uncle Ray, were happy to be in warm and sunny St. Augustine, Florida, on January 22, 1947. It was snowing when they left Baltimore City. They were in Florida because Mom was giving birth to me. All five pounds six ounces of me was born in Flagler Hospital. I was born on my mom's mother's birthday, so I was named Penelope. My grandmother had died years before, but Aunt Sophie said that she would have loved sharing her birthday with her first granddaughter. I looked a lot like Mom, with big brown eyes and a turned-up nose. And I looked like my dad because I only had some black peach fuzz for hair.

They weren't in our house fifteen minutes before Dad and Uncle Ray had set up the chessboard in front of the fireplace in the living room. Dad was the president of the local chess club. He had been the president of the local chess club in Maryland. He and Uncle Ray always got lost in the game of chess. There were times when Mom, Aunt Sophie, Aunt Grace, Frank, Billy, and I would go shopping or to a movie while they were playing chess, and return before the game was over. Neither Dad nor Uncle Ray had any idea we had even left.

Our Florida house looked like a Spanish hacienda outside, but inside, it was more like a cape cod. We entered into the house from the white covered front porch on the right side of the house, which had two arches in the front with red tile floors. As we entered the yellow dining room, we could see the huge white living room to the left that held the fireplace that warmed the whole house. Behind the dining room, past the rounded wall, was the Pullman kitchen. All the walls had rounded corners, and there was a huge curved staircase between the living and dining rooms with a square landing where you could pretend you were on stage and sing, act, and dance carefully, lest you fall down the steps. At the top of the stairs were three bedrooms and one bathroom.

We had moved from Baltimore five months before; and Aunt Sophie, Aunt Grace, and Mom were lonely for each other. These three looked nothing alike and were nothing alike. Aunt Sophie had a wasp waist, stood about five feet two inches tall, had saucer-sized brown eyes, red/brown hair, a turned-up nose, and she smelled good—not like a sweet perfume, but with a wonderful musky odor. She had taught music in the Baltimore City schools.

Aunt Grace stood around five feet tall. She was skinny, although she had a tummy, had coarse black hair, and small beady black eyes. She had a speech impediment and was a slow learner. After my grandmother died, Aunt Grace moved in with my parents.

My mother, Elizabeth, was four feet eleven inches tall. Unlike her sisters, she was very chunky. If I weren't her daughter, I might say that she was fat. She had soft brown hair and brown eyes that turned black when she was angry, and a wonderful mouth because it almost always wore a smile. She was a stay-at-home mother and an avid reader.

The next year, my brother, Billy, was born at the East Coast Hospital, weighing in at nine pounds, six ounces. Of course, Aunt Sophie and Uncle Ray visited Florida, again. Billy looked a lot like Dad except that he had a full head of blond hair.

My dad had come to Florida to be a businessman. He owned a liquor store and then a gas station.

At the liquor store, he used to set me up on the counter. He said that the customers would spend a little more time talking with him and his daughter. My dad used to say that you should treat your auto-mechanic and barber as your best friends. When I was little, I can remember being at the barbershop with Dad, Billy, and Mr. Cliff—the barber—when Mr. Cliff would start up the motor for the boat we would be going on to fish. The whole shop turned into a smoky pit. You could hardly see or breathe. My dad ran his store in the same manner. Every day was to be enjoyed.

Also, he had an incident at the gas station. He corralled an alligator with a fence. He said that for a few days, customers would come to see the alligator who would sometimes stand up. But one day, the alligator decided to leave. Dad, for the briefest of moments, thought he would keep the alligator contained; but when the alligator hissed at him, he let him go.

Dad, in his later years, told me that while he was an honest, caring, hard worker, he didn't work very well for himself. He needed a boss. So after five years in Florida, he decided to go home to Baltimore and resume his job as a taxicab driver. He later moved up to dispatcher and bought a few taxicabs.

Our House

We moved to Loudon Avenue in Baltimore City. My dad liked to boast: "We live in a twenty-foot-wide row house." My brothers and I would sit in the wooden glider and in the rattan chairs on the big covered front porch every fall, spring, and summer, laughing, singing, and talking with our neighborhood friends. In the fall, we'd tell scary stories for Halloween. In the winter, Dad and I would sit in his recliner in the living room with the cabbage-rose wallpaper and the red Oriental rug, read stories, and listen to the Hi-Fi. Every evening, Aunt Grace would bring my brothers ice cream or make them a snack; and every evening, without fail, she would take off one of her shoes and arched her throw so that her shoe bounced off my head. My mother would tell her to stop; but even so, every evening, she still bounced her shoe off my head.

My best friend, Nancy, lived next door. She had a dog and two brothers. We spent a lot of time together when she wasn't attending events at the Catholic Church, and I at the Methodist Church. Sometimes, I went to some of the Catholic children's events. I also liked to read and was happy just hanging out with my dog, Asta.

Nancy and I looked alike—brown hair, brown eyes, medium build, medium height—until we were fourteen years old. Nancy then zoomed to almost six feet tall. Her bedroom was purple, the walls, the rug, the curtains, the ceiling, even the lampshade. It was in this purple room that we learned to smoke cigarettes. We coughed, hacked, and wheezed together. We also learned how to air-out a room in five seconds.

In front of our home was a sign in the shape of the Isle of Wight in Great Britain. My mom said that her family originated from there. There is an Isle of Wight in Ocean City, and I believe that's where she got the sign. But it's true that the Taylor's originally came from the British Isle.

Past the sign, up three steps, and we entered the huge covered wooden porch with white wooden handrails. Open the screen and front door, and we stepped into our house through the foyer where the piano and the organ sat.

Almost every day, our family would sing in the foyer while Frank played the piano. He played hymns primarily, and Billy and I would jump around and dance to them. Yes, he jazzed them up, and we danced accordingly. As for the singing, my brothers and I could never understand how my mother's singing made you want to close your eyes and listen, while my dad's singing made you want to cover your ears.

Past the organ and piano were the stairs to the bedrooms and underneath them, the stairs to the basement. To the side of the stairs you passed over the furnace grate into the eat-in kitchen. It was there that Aunt Grace fixed wonderful meals. But then, there was the night she fixed a fish and left its head on. The eye stared at us, so not one of us three children ate any of it. I don't think Mom and Dad or Aunt Grace ate too much of it either. Even Dad said, "It's staring at us."

It was in this kitchen that I poured chocolate syrup into every glass and bowl. I still don't know why I did it, and Mom would not let me clean it up. I had to sit in the chair in the living room while she and Aunt Grace cleaned up my mess. I really felt like a heel.

At the back of the kitchen was the door to the yard outside. There was a painted-green cement porch with metal poles for the handrails. Three steps down would put you in the garden which consisted of side strips of grassed yard and a beautiful round brick patio with a strawberry pyramid in the center. Both of my brothers bought a few bricks every day from a hardware center and installed them, covering the center yard. Frank bought three metal strips that went around in a circle, the biggest circle filled with dirt on the bottom, with the next circle slightly smaller than the first, and finally the third tier smaller than the second. He filled it with strawberry plants, and every year, we ate strawberries by the handful. This was Asta's domain, along with the rest of the house he shared with Figaro. He was a rat terrier dog—smart, loving, and quite handsome.

Asta

Asta had soft brown ears that sort of folded in half and big round brown eyes. His head was brown with a white strip that ran from the top of his head, between his eyes, down to the black flat bulb at the end of his nose. He had white fur with brown and black spots on the top of his back, and a long brown tail with the end of the always-wagging tail being white.

Asta and I went everywhere together. Every day, we walked to Edmondson Village. There was a library on the right end of the L-shaped shopping center with a movie theatre in the basement. At the intersection of the L, there was a men's barbershop with monkeys climbing on tree limbs in the window, and to the left of that, a brick doggie watering bowl with a spigot you could use to fill up the bowl.

Back Inside Our House

Going back inside, in the kitchen, we turned right to enter the dining room. It comfortably held a china closet, a sideboard, and a table with ten chairs.

Almost every Sunday, Mom and Dad hosted Aunt Helen and Mr. Bost. Dad would pick them up from their row homes in Baltimore City. We picked up Mr. Bost first. He was about five feet eight inches tall and sort of portly. He had a handsome face, with green eyes, black/gray hair, and bushy eyebrows. Billy and I would wait with Dad in our car while Mr. Bost would lock the four locks on his front door at least four or five times before he got in the car with us. He probably just wanted to make sure they were locked, but he was in his eighties, so who's to say? Maybe he couldn't remember.

We then picked up Aunt Helen who was around the same age as Mr. Bost. Mr. Bost would walk to her door and with her back to the car. Aunt Helen, related somehow on Dad's side, was quiet and always kind; but Mr. Bost bothered her a little because he was loud and liked to talk with Aunt Helen. I'm not sure, but I think he was smitten with Aunt Helen who was three inches taller than Mr. Bost, slim with blue eyes, and not very wrinkled, still sort of pretty.

When we arrived home, we would have dinner; and almost every Sunday, Aunt Sophie and Uncle Ray would join us for dinner. Aunt Sophie was Mom and Aunt Grace's sister, and Uncle Ray was her husband. After dinner, we would talk and laugh first about what Frank, Billy, and I were doing and then always about the "old days."

After dinner, Dad returned Aunt Helen to her home first and then Mr. Bost to his house, who did the same locking routine when we took him home. You could hear him turn the locks from inside his house. When the locks stopped turning, Dad would yell, "You okay?" and Mr. Bost would yell back, "Yes!"

Figaro

The dining room was also where Figaro, our blue seal point Siamese cat, used to jump from the china closet onto people who either didn't like cats or who were afraid of them. We really had to be careful when having guests over because Figaro loved to scare anyone who was afraid of him. We never knew how he knew, but he just knew.

Figaro had almond-shaped blue eyes, large pointy upright ears, and was slim and trim. His face around his eyes was medium to dark brown. All four of his legs were dark brown. His body was light brown, almost white, and he had a long dark-brown tail.

Figaro was hard to keep as an indoor cat. He frequently escaped. I recall one evening, around eight o'clock, seeing and hearing a howling dog running down the front sidewalk with a screeching cat having his claws on four stretched-out legs sunk into the dog's back. It may have been funny if it weren't so awful.

Figaro also had an incident with our yellow canary. We kept Yellow Belly Sapsucker in a large cage which hung next to the sideboard. We covered his cage with a cloth every evening and removed the cover in the morning. After about three years, we found Figaro, in the morning, lying on the sideboard with a few of Yellow Belly Sapsucker's feathers near his body. The cover was on the floor, but we never found Yellow Belly Sapsucker.

We had entered Figaro in a pet competition sponsored by Baltimore City. We entered him in the best-looking competition. He looked exactly like he was supposed to. The big bonus was that he kept himself clean and presentable looking. He got the first place in the first three competitions. One more and he would be the winner. We were excited. Dad didn't think about the competition, or I'm sure he would never have put out Figaro the night before. Figaro came home a bloody mess and had a hole in his right ear. No one was happy. Dad, trying to save face, suggested we put an earring in his ear. Needless to say, Figaro didn't win. He got the same as all of the other cats, except for the winner. He got an honorable mention.

Beyond the dining room and next to the hall in the living room was where we put our first television. It had a black and white picture. It was a huge box with a tiny screen—five by seven inches, maybe? One of the television shows required a plastic film that adhered to the face of the television so we could save the cartoon figure, Winky Dink and his dog Woofer, on their adventures. The film made the screen look green. There was a special crayon that we could use to draw a bridge or whatever was necessary to save Winky Dink.

The theme song was: "Winky Dink, and you! Winky Dink, and me! Always have a lot of fun together! Winky Dink, and you! Winky Dink, and me! We'll be pals in fair or stormy weather!"

Between the stairs and on the other side of the living room wall was the grate for the furnace. This was where the heat for our whole house came. In the winter, we would stand over the grate and in seconds, dry off and get warm. When the furnace was on, if you stood over the grate wearing a billowy dress, the skirt would blow up in the air. It was fun to try to hold down the skirt and pretend to be Marilyn Monroe. You had to be careful, though, because you could get burned if you weren't careful.

From the living room, you could enter the hall, walk over the grate, and then climb down the stairs to the unfinished basement where Frank and Billy would work on their train platform year round. Frank was tall, so he could work on the garden without having to use a ladder. He would wear his glasses that framed his large round brown eyes that matched his short brown hair so that he could see to install the electric lights. They had villages and lights that actually lit up the houses and the streets. They had trains and tunnels of course, and they had ice skating figures and mirrors with "snow" for the skaters. They had horses and carriages, and just about every fun winter scene you could think of. It took up half of our basement.

In this unfinished basement also was the ping-pong table where my youngest brother, Billy, so thin you could hardly see him when he turned sideways, would let me win one game a year, always on my birthday.

Upstairs, there were four bedrooms. Aunt Grace had the first one. She had tons of dolls on shelves lining all of her walls. Some were just like the eighteen-inch American Girl Dolls of today, except that they wore clothes from all of the foreign countries as well as from the different areas of America. They were beautiful, and she kept them in pristine condition. I didn't know this for sure, but I believed that she and Mom still played with those dolls.

Mom and Dad had the second room. It was here that our cat, Figaro, placed the rabbit he'd killed in my mother's slipper. It wasn't until she'd put her foot in the slipper that she realized there was a bloody, squishy dead rabbit in there. I can still remember her screaming while trying not to scream. After all, Figaro was just being a good cat. He'd brought home dinner.

Then there was the white-walled bathroom with the white bathtub with the claw feet. We had a white shower curtain that hung from the ceiling and circled the tub. Then there was a white toilet between the tub and the sink, and the white medicine cabinet above the sink. The whole floor was white tile. It was here that I learned to shave my legs and to put small pieces of toilet paper over my razor cuts.

Next was Frank and Billy's room. Billy had a twin bed, and Frank had a full-sized bed. There was still room for chests, dressers, and a desk. It was here that on every Saturday night, the three of us slept together in Frank's bed after the scary television shows, *The Crypt* and *The Outer Limits,* were over.

The last room was mine. It had pink flowers and pink striped wallpaper, and a blue linoleum rug from when I was a toddler with the Cow that Jumped over the Moon and Little Bo Peep, and other assorted fairy tale pictures on it. Under the window sat my hope chest where I could sit and read by the window. All in all, it was an excellent room.

The last in the circle of doors next to my room was the closet with the mirror on the door. I remember singing while twirling in front of the mirror in my new purple Easter dress with the long dark purple ribbon belt, and Figaro was trying to capture my belt while Asta barked loudly. I wonder if he was complaining about my singing?

When I was about twelve years old, standing in the hall, I screamed that Billy was beating on me. My dad came up the steps and made him go to his room. The only thing wrong was that he wasn't beating up on me. I was just mad at him. Even though I was a brat, I did love both of my brothers.

Until Billy went to kindergarten, Mom didn't work outside our home; but when we started school, she went to work in an office. She had stayed home with Frank who was then around eighteen years old. I don't believe our parents needed the money; although I'm sure it was appreciated. Most of the time, Aunt Grace lived with us, and she did the housework. I believe Mom wanted to try something new while Billy and I were at school all day. She enjoyed working with the ladies in the office and, together with Dad, liked socializing with them and their husbands after work occasionally. She got promoted a few times, but she only worked about three years before she had her first heart attack.

Summer Fun

In the summer, we would go to Atlantic City. My dad's company, the Yellow Cab, had an apartment there which the employees could use at any time, except for the month of July when Mr. Reston, the boss, used it. Our family went for a week every June and in August. The apartment was large with two bedrooms. It was spacious, clean, was on the boardwalk, and had a great view of the ocean.

We used the service elevator a lot because it opened up on the boardwalk while the main elevator opened on the front door, at the driveway.

I don't know how I managed to do it, but lots of times we went, I was sick: chickenpox, upset stomach, whatever. I can remember my mom sort of hiding me to the apartment in the service elevator. I also remember coming home on pillows because I got sunburned each year. You'd think I would learn to put on some sunblock instead of the baby oil and iodine mixture we used in those days to get a tan, or in my case, a burn.

Billy, Frank, and I used to walk from the Warwick Apartments to Capt. Starnes, which was at the other end of the boardwalk. I believe that today, it's the Harris Casino by the Bay. We rode bikes on the boardwalk almost every day.

In early July, our family would go to Atlantic City with our cousins: Eddie, Sarah, Cousin Lilly, and Cousin Will. We stayed at the New Belmont Hotel.

It was a really old hotel, and we wondered why it was called the *New* Belmont.

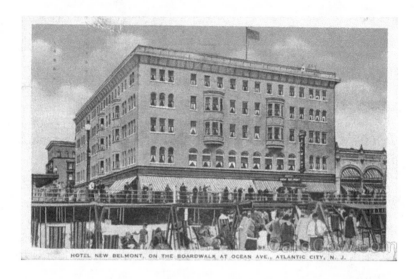

HOTEL NEW BELMONT, ON THE BOARDWALK AT OCEAN AVE., ATLANTIC CITY, N. J.

It was here, on the boardwalk at the Steel Pier, where we saw the diving horse with the pretty lady sitting on him when the horse slid down the sliding-board ramp into the water. We also saw the world's top entertainers and novelty acts. Cousin Lilly liked Bobby Rydell (the '60s teen idol) and was tickled the year he performed at the Steel Pier.

It was also near Planters Peanuts. Outside, there was a man dressed up in a peanut costume who handed out samples of the roasted peanuts. That was Mr. Peanut. We would also go see the Ice Capades at the Convention Center.

Mom and Cousin Lilly loved to sit in the rocking chairs on the porch of the New Belmont Hotel and watch the people go by. They also loved to attend the auctions on the boardwalk. We had more figurines than the law allowed from those auctions. And the horror of the figurines was that they had to be taken down from the shadow boxes and washed each year.

After Atlantic City, Aunt Grace, Billy, and I would go to Uncle Edwin's farm until mid-August. Uncle Edwin was Eddie and Sarah's grandfather, Cousin Lilly's dad, and Cousin Will's father-in-law. Cousin Will always called Uncle Edwin by his last name, Mr. Evans. He owned a tobacco farm. He had horses, cows, pigs, and lots of chickens. He also had the smartest dog ever born. I'm sure Uncle Edwin had a lot to do with her smarts because he trained her. She never wore a leash. She didn't need it. She tried to be intuitive to his wishes. If he needed to tell her something, she did it. She was a Collie, just like in the TV show, *Lassie*, only I think she was smarter. He named her Lassie for the TV show dog.

After a few summers together, Uncle Edwin was killing some chickens for dinner, and the boys chased us with chicken heads and a dead mouse they'd found somewhere. After that, the boys spent their time at the farm separate from the girls, which probably saved Aunt Grace's sanity.

It's quite interesting how they kill the chickens. There are different ways to do it. You can wring their necks or other methods. Uncle Edwin chopped off their heads with a hatchet on a small tree stump. Once you chop off their heads, they flop around; and when they stop, you hang them from clothesline material so they can bleed out. After that, you dunk them in super-hot water and pluck off their feathers. You can then cut them up and cook the meat however you'd like. I preferred fried chicken, but...

At dinner, Aunt Grace would make chicken potpie, and she would always put a chicken foot on top. Sarah, Eddie, Billy, and

I would always have spaghettis on that night. I still wonder if the adults ate the foot, or if they just put it on top to tease us. People do eat pickled pigs feet all the time. I wonder if they pickle chicken's feet? There wouldn't be very much meat on a chicken foot.

Speaking of chickens, one year, a chicken chased me. I remember her wings flapping and her screeching. Finally, Uncle Edwin pulled her off as she was pecking on my back. I don't remember what I did to upset her, but I was sorry I did it.

Billy had a better time with the chickens. Every morning, he'd go out to the hen house and get his eggs from under a chicken. He could also milk a cow, but I never got the hang of it. What a show off!

Billy, my cousins Sarah and Eddie, and I had wonderful times. We were elementary school aged and enjoyed being together most of the time. Sarah was the youngest, then Billy, then Eddie, and then me as the oldest. All four of us were slim as children. One of the niftiest things was that Eddie and Sarah had red hair—that beautiful red/brown hair that was a warm strawberry-blond color. Aunt Grace came with us. She had come for many years with Frank and then with us.

Cousin Lilly and my mom looked a lot alike. Both had black hair, beautiful brown eyes, stocky builds, stood around five feet tall, and they usually were smiling. Likewise, Cousin Will and my dad were both tall and slim, standing somewhere around six feet tall; but while Dad had only fringe black hair, Cousin Will had a full head of black hair.

Mom and Cousin Lilly were always on a diet. How well I remember the grapefruit diet. Dad lost the two or three pounds he'd wanted to lose in two or three days. I can still hear my mom saying, "Bernie, it's just not fair." She, of course, lost at a much slower rate, and usually not much, if any at all. I recall Mom and Cousin Lilly eating cabbage sandwiches for snacks at night. One slice of buttered bread, a huge mound of leftover cabbage from dinner, another slice of buttered bread, and they enjoyed two or three of them at a sitting. Although, I do recall Cousin Will saying at dinner one night that he had to flap the sheets to find Cousin Lilly because she'd lost so much weight. I understood their pain because I've had their weight loss/ weight gain experiences.

Sarah and Eddie's house was a cape cod with a sweeping front yard, side driveway, and steps that entered the back porch at the kitchen in the back of their house. They actually had a basement garage, and you could climb the garage stairs to the hall in the middle of the living room and the kitchen. It was in their kitchen that Billy and I learned the art of eating crabs. Cousin Will, Eddie, and Billy would go to the pier at the creek and catch the crabs. Cousin Lilly would steam them. Crabs should only be steamed, never boiled. Sarah said, "When Mom steamed the crabs, she always used the special seasoning Dad mixed up, which consisted mainly of Old Bay and a few extra spices."

Sarah and I would cover the table with lots of newspapers and napkins, crab mallets, and knives. Everyone would bring their drinks when they came to the table. Cousin Lilly would cover the newspapers with lots of crabs, and we would all grab one. We would twist off the legs, one at a time, and eat any meat that came at the end of the leg and claws (the two in the front). We would start our crab trash pile with the legs, keeping the claws for later. We would turn our crab on its back. Then we would take our knives and pry up the apron (which looks like a thin long white devil's finger). We would slowly pull off the top shell—left to right worked good. We'd scrape off the weird-looking gills (also called devil fingers)—*never* eating them. Other than the devil fingers, the shell, and the cartilage in the claws, everything else, including the crab guts, is edible and delicious. We would break the crab's back in half to make it easier to pick out with the knife or our fingers the crabmeat from the shell chambers. Mmm, mmm. Good!

One of the best parts of eating crabs was the cleanup. We would gather up the newspapers around the crab trash, slide it into a trash bag, and place it in the trashcan. Another best part of eating crabs is that it takes a while to eat them; and while you're eating, you're talking, laughing, and just plain having fun.

Then there was one time that Sarah and I went to the kitchen about three o'clock in the morning to eat leftover crabs. Her dad,

Cousin Will, heard the noise and came out with his shotgun to check on things. Sarah said, "We were lucky he was a cautious man and not the excitable type." I agreed.

On Sundays, we'd swap for Uncle Edwin's (Eddie and Sarah's grandfather, Pop Pop's) house. When we would ride up to Uncle Edwin's farm in Anne Arundel County, only a few miles from the Calvert County line, it was almost like going back to the beach. As we rode down the driveway of crushed oyster shells, the first sight you would see were the gorgeous huge blue hydrangea bushes that surrounded Uncle Edwin's huge porch on his beautiful white two-story with green shutters farmhouse.

You would not notice right away the lovely huge dahlia garden to the right of his house. Uncle Edwin's dahlias stood at least four to five feet tall. I have never seen any dahlias like them since. Some years back, I bought dahlias in a pot—guaranteed to grow big and strong, able to withstand huge winds, blah, blah, blah. Some of them grew only one foot tall. None of them was over two feet tall. I finally found a bulb that was supposed to be enormous. It did get to about three feet high, and it was a pretty blue, but I was looking for more. I guess I needed to have Uncle Edwin's green thumb.

Another thing you didn't see upon arrival was the huge screen porch in the back where Sarah and I used to rock in the rocking chairs and sing songs. "John, Jacob, Jingleheimer Schmidt. His name is my name too. Whenever we go out, the people always shout, 'There goes John, Jacob Jingleheimer Smith.' Tra, la, la, la, la, la, la, la." And of course, "One dark night when we were all in bed, boom, boom, boom. Old Lady Leary lit a lantern in the shed, and when the cow kicked it over, she winked her eye and said, 'They'll be a hot time in the old town tonight.'" It might be a slight exaggeration, but we had a million other songs just like them. And we'd sing them loud.

But not too loud because we always listened for the Good Humor ice cream truck that would come by every day. Sarah considered her Pop Pop's farm on that little narrow dirt road even more "country" than where her family lived, but her family's house never had one ice cream truck pass by.

One of the games we played all of the time was croquet. A sport that involved hitting wooden balls with a mallet through wickets (wire hoops) set in the grass. We'd start at a wooden stake, where we'd hit the ball with a mallet through the wickets in sequence, hitting stakes halfway and then winding back through the wickets to the original stakes, finishing, hopefully, first. It was a lot of fun to play, and everyone won some of the time.

We spent many evenings in Uncle Edwin's huge front yard catching lightning bugs. We each had a jar with a screw-on lid that had holes poked in them so the lightning bugs could breathe, and grass so the lightning bugs would be comfortable. We let them go after we finished catching them. We said that the lightning bugs in the jars were like lanterns. It was fun to see the lightning bugs' lights, but they didn't give off much light.

Billy and Eddie used to follow the farmhands around. They even helped at harvest time. They got to drive the tractor and to cut a row or two of tobacco. They helped put the metal spears on the long wooden sticks when they speared the tobacco and even got to hang some of the tobacco sticks in the barn so the tobacco could dry. They never got high in the barn to hang the sticks. The experienced farmhands did that. It was all hard to do, but it was particularly hard when you were high up, because it was really hot, and the nicotine ran down your arms and was sticky.

Most of the time, Eddie and Billy played catch while they talked about baseball players and baseball in general. Now and then, we would all go to Huntington, where they had a ball field, and watched people play baseball.

Something else the boys loved to do was to go to the "branch" (stream) and to catch tadpoles. There really is nothing better than sitting with your feet in the branch during a hot summer's day.

Lots of days, Sarah and I would wander around the farm. We always took provisions with us, just in case we got lost or something. We always carried a can of spaghettis. We had no can opener, but we felt very safe, and we always found our way home.

Two or three times each summer, Uncle Edwin would drive us in his black '51 Chevy the mile or so to Mr. Walke's store. Mr. Walke looked a lot like Uncle Edwin because he had white hair and was tall and thin. There was one gas pump out front. Inside was a—new at the time—Coca Cola dispenser machine. There was also penny candy and a huge sour pickle jar that was on top of the counter.

Sarah and I were interested in the penny candy and the sour pickle, but Billy and Eddie particularly liked to work the Coke machine, which had two round metal rails on which the small Coke bottle slid that bent down when the money lever was twisted. But you had to get the bottle out quick, or the rail would go back to its original position and the Coke bottle would not come out.

There was a wooden bottle rack that set on an angle to put the empty bottle in when you finished drinking. If you took the bottle with you, you had to pay a deposit, which you received when you returned the bottle. There were no plastic bottles then. The used glass bottles were sent back to the factory, washed, rinsed, sterilized, refilled with Coca Cola, and reinstalled in the Coke machine.

We visited our country relatives during our summers. We had a Hopkins University Professor, George Neuman, as a cousin. When Mount Harmony Methodist Church requested monetary help to maintain the church property, he prepaid for perpetual maintenance on the church property. Aunt Sophie and Aunt Grace's bodies are both buried there, so I have a warm spot for him in my heart.

We had a cousin, Lance Gull, whom I thought was particularly handsome. We would see him and his family each year at their family reunion when we went to Chesapeake Beach. We swam and we played the slot machines. Any age could play the slots back then. Billy seemed to hit all of the time while I never won. Sometimes, he'd give me some of his winnings so I could play a little longer. He was a good guy even then. Billy's most vivid memory of the reunions was one year when a lady changed from her street clothes to her swimming suit while on the beach.

We had a wonderful Cousin Mary and her husband, Steven, who worked at the local lumberyard. One week when our parents and Frank were visiting, we visited their farm for lunch. They grew peanuts and were really wonderful people, but Cousin Mary was a lousy cook. One time, when she asked if we enjoyed the meal, Frank said, "Yes, everything was wonderful. I particularly enjoyed the potato salad." Guess what? Cousin Mary gave him another help-ing. Billy, Sarah, Eddie, and I kept straight faces as Frank consumed the dreadful potato salad. And yes, we teased him about that for the rest of his life, but we never said anything to Cousin Mary even when she moved to Grantly Street which was across from Aunt Sophie who lived on Edmondson Avenue in Baltimore City.

At Uncle Edwin's, we used to sleep in Aunt Clara's room in a huge bed with a pillow that went across the whole width of the top of the bed. We had a chamber pot on the floor because there was no indoor plumbing. We also had a large closet, and we wondered if Aunt Clara's ghost was in there. She died at home and was laid out in the living room. That was how they did it in those days. Sarah and I believed her ghost was in the closet, because when we said what we thought, no one opened the closet. All Uncle Edwin said was that Aunt Clara would not hurt us. I grant you he was probably grinning when he said it.

No indoor plumbing meant we used the outhouse. It was a two-seater, and that meant you could chitchat while doing your business. You had to be careful when using the outhouse because one time, one of us got stung by a bee. On the wall, there was a corncob inside a glass picture frame, just in case you ran out of toilet paper. Funny thing about the cob was that when I was older, my dad told me that Uncle Edwin got the corncob from a souvenir shop in Atlantic City.

Each evening, Aunt Grace got a bucket of cold water from the well and scrubbed the dirt off us. We didn't think that was fun, but we were clean!

One day, there was a black snake on the ground in front of the stable. The stable at one time had been a garage and was converted into a stable with two stalls for the two horses. They were work-horses, not usually the kind that you'd ride on, but they were still fun to pet and feed the occasional carrot.

Eddie still talks about when he and Billy did ride one of the horses, double and bare back (no saddle), a couple of times. That stopped when a dog ran out of the weeds in front of the horse. The horse reared up, and Billy and Eddie slid off. Billy's arm was hurting, and Uncle Edwin took him to the hospital in Prince Frederick. His arm was broken, and a doctor put it in a cast.

Black snakes lived in the loft of the stable. They used to hang from the rafters, and if you weren't careful, you might run into one now and then. One day, somehow or another, one fell out. Black snakes won't hurt you, and they take care of eating the mice and rats. We left him alone and he slithered somewhere. We never saw him again, or at least I didn't think so.

Once, Billy and Eddie were going to be blood brothers. They were each going to cut their finger and then hold them together. But they were both afraid to cut themselves. Billy went to the house and came back with a bright red finger. Eddie said he was surprised and aghast, until Billy told him it was ketchup.

We used to watch the black and white television at Uncle Edwin's (wrestling, baseball, and the *Laurence Welk Show*). Uncle Edwin told us kids one time about one of his neighbors who shot his television with his shotgun because he was angry with the wrestling referees. It did seem wrestling was faked, and the referees never saw half of the stuff the wrestlers pulled. But still, we all got a good grin thinking about the neighbor.

Not only did we spend a lot of time in the country and in Atlantic City, but we also liked to take a cruise or two every summer. Our country cousins and we, city cousins, used to sail on the Wilson Line's Bay Belle boating cruise that sailed around the Baltimore City harbor.

It also sailed to Betterton and Tolchester on the Eastern Shore. The Bay Belle would sail to and dock at Betterton, and we would play the amusement games. Then the Bay Belle would sail to and dock at Tolchester, and we would swim in the water. On the way to and from these stops, musicians would play while the Bay Belle sailed. Our mothers would pay Eddie and Billy to dance with Sarah and I. The cruise only cost $1.50, and they would pay the boys 50 cents each. What a scam, but it was the only way to get them to dance with us.

When I was eleven years old, Cousin Lilly gave birth to Sarah and Eddie's new brother, Joe. He was cute, but he was a baby. My mom died that year, so that was our last summer together. Cousin Will and Cousin Lilly have passed on; but we enjoy getting together with Eddie, Sarah, and Joe every ten years or so. And Sarah and I keep in touch through e-mail.

Mom

My mom died when I was eleven years old.

I can remember the sign on the bathroom mirror, which read, "Don't get the children up. They're not going to school today." Frank was asleep, lying across his bed with his clothes on. Billy was asleep as usual. Aunt Grace was still in her room. I heard Dad in the kitchen, so I went downstairs. His eyes were red, swollen, and sunken looking. He grimaced a smile at me and patted my head. It was then I realized my mother was missing. For some reason, I knew she was not at the hospital. I wondered if she was dead, but that was something I didn't want to think about—out loud anyway. Dad said we should take a walk. Dad and I must have walked around the block of our row home for at least fifty times that morning. He never told me Mom died. He just waited for me to figure it out. I would ask questions, but I never asked if she had died. Lots of times, Mom went to the hospital for heart attacks, but she had been home for quite a while. In those days, heart attacks meant lying in bed. Not like today, when they get you up to exercise the next morning.

When I was about eight years old, my mother had her first heart attack. She had several of them and spent weeks at a time in bed. My dad set up a hospital bed and potty-chair between the living room and the dining room so she wouldn't have to go up and down the stairs, and she could spend her time with our family. I spent a lot of my time sitting on Mom's hospital bed when she was home. It was there that I learned to tell time with the paper clock the school had sent home with me and where I played dolls with my mom. She loved playing dolls. Me, not so much. But I loved her, so I played. I remember she used to check on Billy and me at night when we were in bed. After she died, people told us that her checking on us probably didn't help her. I don't think that hurt her; I think it probably helped her. After all, she loved us, and she was carefully climbing the steps and, in general, moving around.

The funeral home person came to our house and explained the process of American death. They took one of Mom's blue dresses. They cut the sides and laid it on top of her, which made it a shroud. Mom was forty-seven years old. She was laid out for three days and two nights. Two reception sign-in books were filled. Just before closing the coffin, my dad picked me up and said, "Kiss your mother good-bye." I kissed her cheek and that was when I knew for sure that that was not my mother anymore. It was like kissing an icy winter sidewalk. My mother was warm, not like the cold hard thing in that box.

After Mom died, we talked and cried and made a weekly trip to the cemetery to put flowers on her grave, but our daily lives didn't really change very much. Aunt Sophie tried, and with a measure of success, to mother me. I would stop by her house every day after school for an hour or so, talk over the events of our day, and reminisce about Mom. She and Uncle Ray still came to visit us at our house several times a week.

We were sad that Mom died; and my dad, brothers, Aunt Grace, and I relied heavily on Aunt Sophie for support. She was as sad as we were, but she tried to help us cope with Mom's loss. I recall her saying that the good die young and that she was three years older than Mom. Aunt Sophie had been a music teacher. She had a husband, but they never had any children, and she always was close to Mom and treated us like her own. She and Mom took turns taking care of Aunt Grace. Aunt Grace mostly stayed with us, but now and then, she would get mad at my dad and go to stay with Aunt Sophie. After she was there a few weeks, she would get mad at Uncle Ray and come back to stay with us. Aunt Grace was as strong as a horse. I can remember her lifting the leg of the piano and vacuuming under it.

No, Not Again

About fifteen months after Mom died, Aunt Sophie got sick and had come to stay with us for a few days. She slept in my bed, and Aunt Grace and I were glad to take care of her. One afternoon, she asked me if I would fix her a tomato sandwich. Of course, I would. I fixed it just like she liked it—toast with mayonnaise, lightly salted/peppered, thinly sliced tomatoes, with the sandwich cut into fourths. When I returned to my bedroom, I found that she had died in my bed. I was so angry. My mom died the year before, and now Aunt Sophie was gone. I started to scream. How could this be? It was then that I felt Jesus standing next to me. I calmed down immediately. I felt better, but I was still hurt and sad, and all of the other emotions that went along with loss.

Aunt Sophie was buried in Southern Maryland in the church graveyard next to her parents. I did not kiss her good-bye, but I cried more over my aunt than my mother. I felt truly alone. After Aunt Sophie's death, I came home directly after school. Uncle Ray moved out of state, and we never saw him again.

Dad and Frank were arguing all the time. Dad bought a new-to-him 1957 Nash Rambler. The Rambler was the new compact car in the '50s. His was black and white. I remember Dad showing Frank the car, showing off the front seats that reclined, when Frank shouted that the car looked like a skunk, turned around, and left Dad standing there.

Billy and I never had a kind word, let alone a smile for each other.

Aunt Grace, who was always pretty much a background person, became loud and abusive in her language with my dad in particular, but all of us in general. Even my best friend, Nancy, said I was too quiet and too disagreeable to be around and stopped coming over.

Coming Together

After a few weeks, Frank decided that we should take a trip across the United States. Dad said he didn't want to go. He never was much for traveling. So we got ready. We packed our bags and loaded the hatchback station wagon car with sleeping bags and with junk food. As we were saying goodbye to Dad, he informed us that he was going with us. Aunt Grace was staying home, so Dad decided to come with us. Dad's idea of traveling was getting wherever you were going and coming home as quickly as possible, so we were a little worried. But he was glad to be with us, and we had three weeks of quality time together.

The first two days in the car, hardly anyone spoke to anyone else; but as we traveled along, we started talking without straining our lungs. And every now and then, a smile would pop up on one of our faces.

The third day of our trip, the car in front of us hit another car, and the passenger of the car flew out of his door and bounced in the road, in front of our car. Frank somehow rode around the passenger, missing him and all of the cars, so we kept on going. Dad, beaming with pride, said to Frank, "Good job, son."

Frank, grinning all over himself, said, "Thanks, Dad."

On the way home, we actually spoke to one another in caring tones. We traveled to the new at that time—Disneyland in California through the western states and returned home through the southern states. We visited some gold mines—the kind meant for tourists. We have a picture of Billy trying to walk upright because the gold mine had been structured so that you could only walk sideways. It was said that the mine was haunted.

We spent our first night in California next to an orange grove. It was late and we couldn't find a hotel. It was here that I put my sleeping bag in the hatchback on top of Dad's hat. He was angry, but what could he do? We couldn't iron it, so he wore it like the rumpled mess it had become. He wouldn't buy a new one. I felt a little guilty/bad, but not so much that I was upset.

Of course, we visited Disneyland, which was spectacular. A really cool thing happened on the way home in Texas. It was pouring down rain, and then it was dry. You could see it was still raining on the back of the car, but it was sunny and dry on the front of the car. We still missed Mom and Aunt Sophie, but we had shaken off that terrible gloom of depression we had sunk into.

We got on with living. Aunt Grace had not wanted to go with us. She probably needed some time alone. When we returned, even though she was stuck with Dad, and he with her, they got along. After our California trip, our lives began to settle into a routine. Frank bought a boat, and he and Billy, with the help of Mr. Ed., Frank's friend from work, spent almost every Saturday doing boat work, sanding and painting or working on the motor. Dad started to date. We had phone calls from all kinds of women, all hours of the day. They ran the gamut from taxi drivers to an opera singer. I stopped with the long face and grumpy attitude, and Nancy and I became friends once more.

Getting Older

That year, when I was twelve years old, Dad gave me a credit card for the Lerner Shop which was a women's clothing store. He said that he didn't want to be involved in my clothes. The only restriction was that I had to give him the bill before it was due so he didn't have to pay interest. He never questioned what I bought nor how much it cost. That was a big help to me. I never bought frivolously, and it was a comfort to know that intimate apparel as well as any kind of clothing could be purchased without questions.

When I was fourteen years old, I got my first boyfriend. Norman was his name. He was somewhat skinny with curly black hair and dark blue eyes. We met at the church youth group, and we dated doing youth group things—hayrides and dances and that sort of thing. On Valentine's Day, he brought me a big box of chocolates; but after he got out of his dad's car, he dropped the box and his dad ran over it. Norman's usually fair complexion turned the color of ashes and then bright pink. He picked up the box and said, "I'm sorry." He shouldn't have worried. The lid was still on and we ate them all.

Cold War

In the middle to late fifties, the Cold War was going on, and everyone was worried about an atom bomb attack. The elementary school #66, where Billy and I attended, sent home a notice to the parents, asking if, in the event of a nuclear attack, they wanted their children to go home, or to stay at school and get under their desks. Every parent—or so it seemed—sent back that they wanted their children to come home, except my dad, who said we should get under the desk. I was really upset with him. He didn't care enough to have us come home? Well, now that I'm older, I realize that he wanted us as safe as we could be; and we would not be safe running the streets with all of the other children trying to get home. Not to mention that if the atom bomb actually hit, it wouldn't matter one way or the other where we were. My dad's theory was that if the bomb did strike us, we should stand outside—right under the bomb—and look up at the beautiful lights.

Continental Can

When we were young, our family went every year to the Continental Can picnic day at Gwyn Oak Park because Dad's brother, Uncle Matt, worked at Continental Can and could get tickets for us too. Mom, Dad, Frank, Billy, and I ate lunch at one of the hundreds of picnic tables. After lunch, the adults liked to play cards at the tables. My brothers and I had so much fun that I will never be able to forget it. They had the roller coaster and a zillion other rides. They had the weight guessers and the age guessers. They had hit the ball and ring the bell. And they had tons of food like cotton candy and funnel cakes. It makes me smile to this day when I think about going there. Hurricane Agnes rumbled through and ruined the park, but it still makes me happy to remember the fun we had there.

Teenage Years

Also around that time, segregation was over, and African American people started to move into the neighborhoods that had been only previously populated by white people.

That's what they say today. The truth is, at least in my neighborhood, the realtors moved two huge black guys in a corner row house. There were no women or children in that house, just the two huge guys. One evening, Asta and I were coming home from Edmondson Village. As we rounded our corner on Loudon Avenue, one of the huge African American guys came running behind me. He was probably just jogging, but I was frightened. After that, I made sure that I was home by dark if I was alone.

After a few months, African American families did move into the neighborhood. The children and I got along. We played on the streets and sang songs on our front porch. We would walk to school together to Edmondson High which was a brand-new school with a swimming pool on the top floor. One of the girls, Yolanda, was in my swim class, and we'd talk about how we'd try to save each other because we were sure we would drown. What's funny about that is that we both ended up with lifesaving certificates. I guess it was worth it, but we had to wear the most awful swimsuits for class. They had different colors, but they were all thin fabric, one piece, hard to get on, and just as hard to get off—and we had to shower together. Thank goodness we were all girls, but even so, I liked showering alone; and I believed all of the rest of the girls did too.

Another wonderful thing that happened at Edmondson High School was that there were so many students that by my fourth/senior year, we went to school in morning and in afternoon shifts. I was an academic major, which meant that I did not take a typing class, and I wanted to learn to type. So I was allowed to take a typing class in the first period of the afternoon shift. In those days, the electric typewriter was new. We had one in our class. When you pressed the keys, the whole machine seemed to jump. We learned to type on the manual typewriter, but when our turn came, it was fun to type on a machine that could move so fast.

Billy attended City High School. They had a rivalry with Poly High School. Our house wasn't a sporting household; but on Thanksgiving Day, every year for four years, we watched City High School play Poly High School and of course, rooted for City.

Frank, many years before us, attended Glen Burnie Senior High School, which meant that all of us attended different high schools.

Asta Died

I was fifteen years old when, coming home from Edmondson Village, Asta was run over by a car.

I called him but did not realize he was across the street. As always, he tried to come.

I never put him on a leash, but I should have. I felt sad for a long time.

Jobs

When I turned sixteen years old, my dad asked me if I knew what day it was. "Yes." It was my birthday. Dad said it also was Work Permit Day, and he took me downtown to obtain my work permit.

The next day, I got a job working for the Tommy Tucker dime store in Edmondson Village. After about a year, the store burned down; and while I was looking for a new job, my dad hired me to work in the Yellow Cab office with him as a bookkeeper, and that was where I worked until I graduated from high school. I liked the job. I collected the manifests from the cab drivers and tallied up the jobs and the fares they made from the jobs. When things didn't add up, I helped the drivers figure up their manifests. My dad was the dispatcher and assigned the drivers to the cabs. We got along well. I learned a lot about my dad. He liked to chitchat with the drivers. He was one of them. He had driven a cab for years. Dad and a few of the drivers owned cabs.

Dad and a lot of the other cab owners had a problem in that they'd bought the cabs when they were worth more than they were worth then. I recall Dad being upset because when he'd decided to retire, he had to take a large loss on his cab investments.

It was because he was a cab driver that he was excommunicated from his church, or so Dad liked to say. Dad's priest told him that he needed to come to church on Sundays. Dad drove several women customers back and forth to church on Sundays. He wasn't going to give up those fares. Dad said that the priest told him that if he didn't go to church, he would be excommunicated. We'll have to take Dad at his word, but it did sound fishy to me. My dad's dad passed on before I was born, which makes me think my dad might not have pulled the religion change if he'd still been alive. My mother had been Methodist when they married, but had embraced the Catholic religion and had taken the classes to be Catholic. Frank was baptized Catholic. My dad decided to be Methodist. His family, his mother, and his brothers and their wives were none too happy with him; and I believe Dad kind of liked being the naughty Christian.

My mother's mother had passed on long before I was born. I was named after her because I was born on her birthday, a fact I found out from the baby book my mom kept for me. I have a picture of my grandmother in her wedding dress. I wasn't sure it was her, but after close examination, I saw she made a beautiful wedding dress. But she hemmed it on, I'll bet, her wedding day. That's something I would do and have done, not with wedding dresses, but with other apparel. It's got to be my grandmother's picture.

Stepmother

Our family had always been close before Mom died and stayed close even when Frank moved out with Aunt Grace after Dad married Henrietta when I was sixteen years old. When you're sixteen years old and you've been without a mother for five years, you don't want a stepmother, particularly one that's not too fond of you or your brothers; but Dad remarried.

Frank and Aunt Grace moved out into an apartment, and we moved to a sixteen-foot row house. The new house was small, but now there were only four of us: Dad, Henrietta, Billy, and me. The best attribute of that house was that it was adjacent to Miss Rita's house. While we didn't begrudge my dad remarrying, we didn't know Henrietta and had only met her a few times. She was somehow related to us—one of those "cousin by marriage, three times removed" relations. She had a son who didn't like "city slickers" like us. He was married and had children of his own, so at least he didn't live with or even near us. Henrietta wasn't exactly mean, but she didn't like having Billy or I around. I can remember having to use Miss Rita's iron and ironing board, because the one in our house belonged to Henrietta, and she wasn't sharing. Our Dad tried to step in now and then, but he wasn't any help to Henrietta or to us. Even with our difficulties in getting along, I was glad Dad had a wife. I felt that I could now have my own life too because before Henrietta, I had decided I would have to stay home and take care of Dad.

At eighteen years old, when I left to go to Frostburg State, Billy left home. We weren't angry, but the family fun was gone, and Billy would be home alone. So he chose to move to New Orleans at age seventeen. He became a cook, got his own apartment, and in general, did very well

You Chase Them Until They Catch You

We met in college at Frostburg State. He was a senior, getting ready to graduate. I was a freshman starting in January. I lived off campus for the second half of the first semester because I started mid-year. I graduated from high school on Friday and started work on Monday at the local Hot Shoppes cafeteria as a cashier. I worked there six months until I got enough money to attend Frostburg State Teachers College. Had I known that my dad was going to give me all of the rent money I'd paid after graduating high school, I might not have saved so heartily, so I'm glad he didn't tell me.

I saw him in the cafeteria line. He was working in the cafeteria. I said to my roommate, Deidra, "I am gonna get a date with that guy." Sure enough, I met him at the dance, and I made sure I was in his area. Patrick was dancing, and I believe he'd had a few beers because he was oblivious to his pants riding down his hips. Today, not many folks would have thought anything about that, but in the '60s it wasn't appropriate. He asked me to dance, and then he asked me out. Woohoo!

It was a match made in heaven. Although he worked in the cafeteria, he did not have a food pass. Using my food pass, I went from, "I'll have a little of that," to "make my helping huge," so he could eat real food instead of what he could beg from his friends. Patrick was six feet one inch tall, weighed 160 pounds, and had black hair with a cowlick that curled up on the right side of his head. I dated him for a month before I realized he had hazel eyes. He usually wore a blue sweater, and I thought his eyes were blue.

He had brought his father's car to school for his last semester. Imagine my surprise when our first date was in the cafeteria alcove where the TV was. We talked through a myriad of TV shows while his friend borrowed the car.

I probably should have been upset, but I just liked being with Patrick even then. Of course, I liked learning about him. I don't think I ever rode in that car. You could walk everywhere you wanted to go in Frostburg. We were young, and it was fun to walk and talk together.

Patrick told me that he had dropped out of Frostburg State and had enlisted in the Air Force two years before. He had hoped to be an airplane mechanic. He completed boot camp and was awaiting his assignment. He said the regulars had to wait for the ninety-day guys to get their assignments first. While waiting, he had some foot problems. They actually had to cut off his boot. The Air Force doctor said he thought Patrick should take the honorable discharge offered from the Air Force. Patrick took the offer and then he signed up again for college at Frostburg State.

After I started dating Patrick, I attended one of his fraternity sandlot baseball games. My "house mother," Mrs. Holmes, who looked just like Aunt Bee on the *Andy Griffith Show*, suggested I make some fried chicken and take it to the game. After all, "A man's heart is through his stomach." That's an old saying that I thought was silly, but I believe it worked with Patrick.

After a couple of months, I was getting a little tired of him, so I was happy when he told me at the close of the semester that that was when school romances end. He graduated and left. He didn't invite me to his graduation. I went home for the summer.

I was home with my hair in giant rollers, getting ready for work as a cashier for the local Hot Shoppes cafeteria when Patrick knocked on our door. Imagine my surprise when he told me he was in the neighborhood and had decided to stop by. He was working for a local factory for the summer. I hadn't seen nor heard from him since school was out, but I must admit, I was glad to see him. We dated the rest of the summer. He had a job in Essex, Maryland, as a teacher, and I had to go back to school.

We wrote letters. We called and made ourselves totally miserable because we were apart. It seems silly now, but it seemed like a huge deal then. I received a letter from my dad which said,

> How's my girl? Hope you are acclimated by now.
> Patrick stopped by Friday and Sunday nites. Poor boy is in bad shape. He misses you so. Sunday nite he said that he was going to do something about it. Such as to get you to marry him *pronto*. So be aware. Don't make any hasty decisions that you may regret. Think about the situation carefully before deciding. You can marry him now or in December, or you can tell him to go fly his kite. However, I am with you all the way, no matter what you decide to do.
>
> Ever loving,
> Dad

Here is where I have to admit that I got Patrick on the rebound. He was engaged to a girl named Lois from school. She broke up with him that winter when they were home on Christmas vacation. I never met her and only saw her from her picture. I believe that Patrick's family was not high enough on the food chain for her and her family. Patrick must have had doubts that there could be more than one woman for him because he took me to see his minister at his church. The preacher was only five or six years older than Patrick, and they had become friends. Patrick introduced me to Pastor John at his parsonage. I didn't know until Pastor John said that, "There's more than one for everyone," that I was being reviewed and okayed by the preacher for Patrick. Patrick tried to give me Lois's engagement ring, but I refused that. I actually wore my mother's engagement ring and wedding ring. Mom would have liked that. I wanted to wait until I had finished at Frostburg, but he wanted to marry that year. I picked the month—December, and he picked the year—1966.

Frank's Family

While we were dating, Frank, my oldest brother, got married. He was working as a secretary for Olin Matheson, a chemical company in Glen Burnie, Maryland, where he met Mia. They married and moved to Frank and Aunt Grace's apartment in Baltimore. Mia became pregnant with a boy who would be named Andrew. We were all looking forward to being aunts and uncles, and grandfathers and grandmothers. But our mood changed when we got the call that Mia had been in labor too long, and something had happened to Andrew's lungs. He wouldn't live long.

Patrick and I went to the hospital to see him. He was beautiful. He looked good to me, but Patrick said, "I think he's supposed to be red." And he wasn't; his skin was pale. He lived one day. Mia insisted on going to the funeral. The doctor said she shouldn't, but I probably would have too. It makes me cry to think about it, even now. My dad used to say, "The worst thing that can happen to you is to lose a child." He would preface that with, "I don't want to know how it feels, but…"

A few days after the funeral, Mia went to the hospital for some psychiatric counseling. She'd spend the week there but would come home on the weekends. So, we were not surprised when she became pregnant again. This time, she had a healthy baby girl named Suzanne. She and Frank were happy and so were we. After Suzanne was six months old, Frank came home from work to find Mia screaming and seemingly going crazy. Her colon had burst. The doctor said that there was nothing that they could have done to save her. She died that evening.

Another Funeral

Mia's twin sister attended the funeral. She looked exactly like Mia—short, slim, brown hair, pretty smile, and a soft voice. Suzanne held out her arms for whom she thought was her mom. I can still picture Mora's tears as she picked up Suzanne. That evening, she left the house and went home to New York. When Suzanne got older, she would go now and then to visit Aunt Mora in New York.

Getting Married

Patrick purchased our first car before we were married. It was a used '62 Chevy, red with black interior—totally radical! It helped show that Patrick loved me. In those days, I smoked; and as I had done many times before, I threw a lit cigarette out of the front passenger's side window. But this time, it flew back into the back window and burned a hole in the middle of the back seat. I felt like the biggest creep on earth. But the damage was done, and I couldn't undo it. Patrick said it was okay, but you could see on his face his heartbreak.

On December 10 of 1966, there was a huge snowstorm; and on December 24, there was another huge snowstorm. But on December 17, while there was lingering snow on the ground, the skies were sunny, the streets were clear, and it was a relatively warm day the day Patrick and I were married. I can still remember walking down the aisle on my dad's arm at Central Summerfield Methodist Church, and he was whispering to me that if I wanted, we didn't have to do this. We could just go home. I couldn't believe he said that. All the money, time, and things we did to get this wedding ready. I had borrowed my sister-in-law's wedding dress, bought white three-and-one-half-inch heels, gone to great lengths to get just the right flowers even though the florist delivered roses in my bouquet when I'd asked for carnations. He did put a carnation in the center, and the bridesmaids had carnations in their bouquets. I was unhappy about the lack of carnations, but when you're getting ready to walk down the aisle, you go with the flowers. Henrietta, my stepmother, and I had made the bridesmaids' flowered headpieces. The ladies of the church had cooked tons of food and prepared the fellowship hall for the reception. And here was my dad saying we could just go home. He was a pretty thrifty guy, and here he was telling me that I was worth more than money. Thanks, Dad.

Frank and his family, had come from West Virginia to help officiate my marriage; and Billy, my youngest brother, had come home for good from New Orleans, Louisiana. My dad loved Billy with all his heart and was lost until he returned for my wedding. So not only did my dad get a son-in-law, he also got back his son.

Right before the ceremony, Brad, Patrick's brother and best man, informed us that he'd forgotten the wedding ring. I wore a size eight-and-a-half ring. Most ladies wear somewhere around a size seven. When I was a girl, my dad used to give me the paper ring off his cigars. If Mrs. Carter, our neighbor, had not lent her ring to one of the ushers so I'd have one for the ceremony, I may have married with a paper-cigar ring.

After the wedding and reception were over, Patrick and I went to dinner at the Hot Shoppes in the Eastpoint shopping center. Then we went home to our apartment in Essex. We didn't have money for a honeymoon, and we really didn't need one. We were happy just being together.

Starting Out

Before we got married, I went to the gynecologist for a checkup. Everything was fine. Before I left, the doctor said that my first night with Patrick would hurt and that he could fix that with two scissor snips. I knew what he was talking about, but my mom always said that virginity was a gift that could only be given once, so I declined the two scissor snips. Many times during our first night, I wished I had agreed. Every time I would complain about the pain, Patrick would stop. Then, after we cuddled a little, we'd be at it again. And in the end, Patrick stood next to me with his arm around my shoulder and proclaimed that that little splatter of blood on the sheet was "your cherry." So I was glad I'd saved the "gift" for him and that he was smart enough to know he'd received a gift. Good call, Mom.

Seven days after we were married, we picked out our first Christmas tree at Cheap Charlie's, located on Essex Boulevard. There's not too much left on Christmas Eve, but we got a beautiful tree. It was five feet tall, so it was small, but it was beautiful in shape and in color. Patrick and I put lights on it, and we put on some decorations. We enjoyed just looking at it. We were the two happiest people on earth.

A few weeks after we were married, I was almost asleep when Patrick yelled, "SBD," and started flapping our blanket. A horrible odor like the smell from hell hung in our bedroom. It was as though multiple garbage trucks invaded our room. I fled to the living room. He came after me wearing a big showy grin.

I asked, "What happened?"

He said that he had farted and that it was an SBD, also known as Silent But Deadly. Lucky him because he got to air out our bedroom. I would like to say that that was his first and only SBD, but that would be a lie. Periodically, throughout our marriage, he would have an SBD, and he would always flap our blanket and smile with pride. Lest you think he's the only guy to do that, know that through the years, he and his male friends used to brag to each other when they had accomplished an SBD.

Patrick and his dad shared the same cost-effectiveness as my dad. The horrible apartment Patrick and his dad had picked out for Patrick when he first started teaching was on the second floor with peeling paint, and it was furnished with furniture and drapes from the 1940s or 1930s. That was when I learned a lesson about home repair. There are some things you can skimp on, but paint is not one of them. I bought green paint from the dime store to cover over the bright paint in our bedroom. I put on three coats, and you could still see the orange. I remember sitting on the bed, crying. Patrick put his arm around me and assured me that he could fix this. No, he was not going to paint; but he did take me to the hardware store where I picked out a medium blue for the kitchen cabinets, another green for the bedroom, and white for the kitchen and living room walls, and the trim paint. Who knew one coat of a premium paint would cover everything? I got some rooster decals for the kitchen cabinet doors. I painted the ceilings white. The walls in the bedroom were a beautiful green, and the living room no longer looked dingy. I bought new drapes, and I washed and folded the old drapes and put them in the closet. I vacuumed the furniture. We were living large!

About a month or so after we were married, we had our first fight. I can't remember why we fought. But I do recall packing my overnight bag, going out the front door, and "leaving" Patrick. So there I was at the top of the stairs because we lived on the second floor, wondering what to do. I didn't want to go home to my dad's house. My home was on the other side of that door, at the top of the stairs with Patrick. It seemed like a long time, but I believe it was only a few minutes when I swallowed my pride and went back through the front door. Patrick was so glad to see me that he hugged me for the longest time. Maybe that's why I have always loved being hugged? I don't know, but I do know that I never "left" Patrick again.

After six months or so, I went to work for the County Recreation and Parks, and spent a lovely summer working on the playground with the students. Patrick worked for the county too, only he scrubbed the school gym floors. But we had plenty of time for fun too. We liked to play tennis. He would hit the ball over the net to me, and I would try to hit it back to him. Every blue moon, when the werewolf howls, we would get it back and forth two or three times. Needless to say, neither one of us was good at tennis, but we did try all summer; and we had fun. We also got a lot of exercise running to get the ball.

After the summer ended, I got a full-time job with a finance company as a sort of secretary. I sometimes helped the collection office by tracking down non-payers. If you need to locate a non-payer, just call their mother. They are usually very forthcoming. The collection guys who went out used to tell me that they didn't have too many problems with family dogs attacking them. It was the children that would kick, bite, and otherwise do them bodily harm.

Different Worlds

My dad was one of the smartest people I have ever known. He only had a sixth-grade school education; although, he would tell his three children repeatedly that he knew his times tables up to twelve before he entered school. He was really good in math, so he probably was not kidding about that. However, he always enjoyed telling us that he did not become an astronaut because he couldn't count backward from one hundred. Yes, Dad was a corny joker. Dad could "read" people. He knew if you needed a hug. When we would go to a funeral home, if no one was crying when he came in, they were all crying when he left. While the only animal I believed he ever loved was his childhood gray wired-haired terrier dog, Wolfgang, when one of your pets died, he would help you bury it and would at least look sad. He was smart too in that he embraced life. When Patrick asked Dad if he'd be okay with our getting married, my dad decided that he was one of the family and treated Patrick as though he were his third son.

No two families could have been more different. Patrick came from a military family, his dad being a Marine Captain, having served for twenty years. My dad was drafted into the Navy in World War II and was glad when his service time was over. As he put it, "Craziness is a man (thirty-six years old) with a wife and son drafted into the Navy." But you could detect some pride when he said that. Patrick loved sports, playing and watching. My dad would rather play chess. He was the Grand Master chess player in Florida and president of the Aaron Chess Club in Maryland. Patrick had the skills of a chess player and was a great mathematician, but he'd rather play ball than sit at a chess table. My dad also enjoyed a libation every day. Patrick might have a beer or two once a year, but he'd much rather have a glass of sweet tea. My dad wore a mustache, and soon after we were married, Patrick grew a mustache. He tried growing a beard, but it made him itch. A little kid usually tries to emulate his dad, and I believe that was what Patrick was instinctively doing. He loved being part of my family, and they loved him being part of our family.

We purchased a new Volkswagen bug. It was the color called zenith blue. We were both working, so we wanted to have two cars, and we were tickled to have a new vehicle. But my dad said, "A Volkswagen is a car that people who can't afford a car buy." We didn't care. We were happy to have an additional vehicle. On one of our trips to Frostburg, while the car was less than one year old, it broke down on the road. Patrick was outside the bug, looking at it, when another motorist stopped by, jerry rigged some sort of wire from the back where the motor was, over the top of the car to somewhere near the trunk in the front. It ran the rest of the way to Frostburg. Thank goodness for that motorist and for Patrick who took care of getting it fixed in Frostburg. We also had another adventure with the bug when we went to visit my dad and Henrietta on her farm. The car just stopped running, and we were stranded, but Patrick called someone who came and worked on it in the yard so that we could ride home in it, and he had it fixed the next day. We rode it back and forth to St. Augustine, Florida, at least ten times; so even though I'm kind of complaining about it, we were happy to have it.

After about a year, Patrick realized that renting a furnished apartment cost more money than renting an unfurnished apartment, so we bought some inexpensive furniture and moved to a first-floor apartment. Some of the furniture stores, including Montgomery Ward, had deals in those days which included three rooms of furniture for a set price. We purchased a living room set with a sofa, three tables, two lamps, and two chairs; a bedroom set complete with a bed, mattresses, two night tables, a chest of drawers, a dresser with a mirror, and two lamps; and a kitchen set with a table and four chairs combination. It was great fun to get all new furniture and a new apartment to paint. Because when we moved, I had to repaint the other apartment back to white, I painted this one all white. That was a good thing because we only stayed there one year.

Towson State College was where I tried to transfer from Frostburg. They made me attend night school, saying I had to earn admission. They also refused to take half of my credits. After all, I had committed the cardinal sin of that time and had married. I remember the counselor at Frostburg being upset when I told her I was going to marry. It wasn't until I tried to transfer that I realized why. I took a couple of courses, but decided I wanted to have my children when I was young so I had a better chance of living to raise them. So I dropped out.

Our Oldest Baby

I wanted to have children, and in February 1968, I became pregnant. I was so excited. Patrick was so worried. Would the baby be okay? Would I die giving birth? We could not stay in a one-bedroom apartment, or so he said, so we rented—in the same complex—a two-bedroom apartment with a living room, kitchen, dining area on the first floor, and two bedrooms and a bath on the second. Then he worried if we would be on the street because the two-bedroom apartment was more money each month. Jeez, Louise!

In June, my dad gave Patrick $100, which was a lot of money in those days. He told Patrick to take me on a vacation. We went to Atlantic City. We stayed one night in a fancy hotel. We sat on the beach and looked in on the auctions on the boardwalk. Because I was five months pregnant, we walked slowly along the boardwalk, talking and laughing, wondering about what kind of parents we hoped to be. That evening, we ate dinner in the fancy hotel where the waiters wore gloves. We were very impressed. We had lots to talk and laugh about while Patrick drove us home the next day.

Margot was born on November 27, 1968. Margot was named by her dad. Patrick had a girl in his sixth-grade class named Margot. She was her own person. She was a little defiant, but still willing to abide by the class rules. She was a critical thinker who didn't need to be taught to think critically. She was intelligent and pretty, just like our Margot. When I looked up how to spell her name, I was surprised that the *t* is silent. I liked that, and I made sure I spelled it right for her birth certificate

She was beautiful. Actually, she still is beautiful—older but beautiful, still. I can remember holding her in my lap, thinking how blessed Patrick and I were while watching our American astronauts on television walk on the moon.

When Margot was about three months old, on a Friday, Patrick suggested we go for the weekend to an event at Frostburg State. That sounded good to me, but I had gone back to work; and there were diapers and regular clothes to wash, and dishes and dirt to clean. The bottom line was I didn't finish everything until Sunday afternoon, so we couldn't go. I didn't think that he thought about getting ready. I had asked Patrick in the past if he would help me with the household chores. He would for a day or so, and then not so much. I decided that if he did one chore all the time, that would be enough to help me. That Sunday, I asked him to pick a chore that he would not mind doing all the time. He picked the clothes. I reminded him that he would have to wash, dry, and put away the clothes. Did he still want to do that chore? "Yes." He did.

When we were first married, Patrick and I went to the laundromat every Saturday, or sometimes Friday if we had a party or other event. We always had two baskets of clothing, and we spent the night washing, drying, and folding clothes while laughing and talking—almost gossiping about our week. After Margot was born, we just used the laundry services in the apartment complex which was okay in that I could throw the clothes in the washer, come back, and throw them in the dryer; but the date-night atmosphere was gone. Patrick knew from firsthand experience what washing the clothes entailed; that it was a big job. Patrick took care of himself so that he always looked neat and clean. I believe this was his way of insuring he always had clean clothes.

The first few times he did the wash, he'd "accidentally" turn my underwear pink, but I was happy to wear pink. When our children were tall enough to reach the top of the washer, he trained them how to wash their clothes. That was okay with me. I didn't have to wash any clothes for the next forty-two years, and in all that time, Patrick never once complained.

Another good thing about Patrick washing the clothes was that it was then okay for me to use throwaway diapers. I can remember Patrick getting up with Margot one night when she woke up crying.

He picked her up but did not change her. He actually never changed either one of his children's diapers. He did hold Margot up in the air when she'd had a bowel movement around five months old. I came home and he handed me her feet, so I changed her.

Neither Patrick nor I were well versed in taking care of children. I babysat when I was a teenager—pre sixteen years old—but none of the "babies" were under five years old. Patrick only watched his youngest brother with Brad, and the few times that they watched him didn't turn out well. One time, on their way home, their parents found Marty walking outside on the sidewalk, wandering around the neighborhood. Another time, Patrick and Brad lost him, but their parents found Marty in their house.

After Margot was born, I went back to work at the finance company. My boss had suggested I use his niece as a babysitter. She came to my house. All seemed great. She redressed Margot every day, but I just thought she liked to dress her up. After one week, I came home and saw my next-door neighbor. She said that Margot cried all day. So I resigned the next day. I have always regretted leaving Margot home with the sitter. I should have checked out the sitter or put Margot in a daycare where there were people, but I didn't. I couldn't undo whatever the sitter had done, so I stayed home with her for the next three years until after we'd purchased our first home.

When I went back to work, I made sure I worked when Patrick was home; or I used Anita, the next-door teenager, as a babysitter for the one-half hour or so between when I left for work and Patrick came home. After a while, I convinced Miss Rita, a lady I loved, who had sold her house to Anita's parents, to watch my children. She had four children, teenagers by then, and there was always someone stopping by and something going on at her house. When it was time for me to go to work, I would drive to her house, open the car door to let the children out, and they would run to her door.

When I came to pick them up, I had to go into the house and have a piece of cheesecake because they made one every day that they went to Miss Rita's. It was a good thing I worked part-time because one can only eat so much cheesecake.

The Brothers Wed

Patrick's brother, Brad, used to visit us several times a week. We had a lot of fun arguing about politics, the state of the nation, the hairstyles of the teenagers, and anything else we could disagree about. Patrick would sit up for a while with us and then he would go to bed. Brad and I would argue for a couple more hours and then he'd go home. He didn't like my sandwiches. Brad said they were too skinny. He'd rather have meatloaf than lunchmeat. It was fun to have a friend—actually a relative—to argue with.

When Brad was in the Marines in Vietnam, he had a good friend who had a sister that he wanted Brad to meet. Brad flew out to California to meet her and fell in love. After a few months, he married Lonnie. She and I got along pretty well. She didn't know anyone from the East Coast, so I got to be her matron of honor. I was pregnant with Lance, so he was at their wedding, but Patrick's parents didn't think it was appropriate for Margot to be there because she was two years old. You know the old saying about toddlers: terrible twos, terrific threes. So Margot missed that wedding, but when she was thirteen years old, she was a bridesmaid in Patrick's younger brother's—Marty and Pepper's—wedding.

Frank's Family Continues

After Mia's passing, Frank, Suzanne, and Aunt Grace moved to West Virginia. Frank got himself a job as a part-time Methodist preacher to two churches in Falling Waters, West Virginia. He took Suzanne and Aunt Grace with him. God took care of him because these two churches took him in with loving arms and took care of him until he died. They gave him his own house and a half-acre of land to put it on. And every growing season, canning season, and hunting season, he got tons of food. While the churches tried to set him up with a wife, he found one on his own. Alice was her name. She had worked in Washington, D.C., but was a farm girl from Chanute, Kansas. Frank and Alice went home to Kansas with Margot and me tagging along. Patrick and Billy stayed home, but we telephoned Patrick every night. I was the chaperone for the trip. We had a good time, and we met, for the first time, Alice's Mom and Dad. Her parents were nice people. Mrs. Alto let Margot and Suzanne do pretty much whatever they wanted, which included scaring the pigs in the pig pen by squealing at them. Jim, Alice's brother, lived at home, and he took Suzanne and Margot all around the farm and saw to it that they had fun. They got to pick corn, wheat, and even ate some soybeans. Jim had two dogs whom Margot and Suzanne fed whenever they had food, which was a lot. They learned a new-to-them song, "Old MacDonald Had a Farm." I recall Mrs. Alto saying that if they needed more money for the wedding or anything else, they'd just sell a cow.

Frank and Alice never had any children, but the four of them got along just fine. Aunt Grace died of old age when Suzanne was eight years old. Frank died with a heart attack just before he was getting ready to retire at sixty-two years old. Today, Suzanne is a well-educated preacher, still working on her doctorate. Alice still works as the church secretary and lives in their home in West Virginia.

Living in the City

A year or so before Billy and I were born, my parents moved from Baltimore to Florida. My dad, always the entrepreneur, bought a liquor store, and later a gas station. They also purchased a home in St. Augustine. They came back to Baltimore after the businesses were unsuccessful, but they had kept the house, so my dad decided to retire to Florida with Henrietta. Patrick and I purchased my dad's row home in Baltimore City that he and Henrietta purchased when they were first married.

I was a teenager when I first lived in this sixteen-foot row house. My friend, Miss Rita and after she moved, my new neighbor/friend Anita lived in the house next door. The alley in the back held special memories for me. I had two dogs growing up. The first died when I was about fifteen years old. His name was Asta, and he was a great dog. He was a rat terrier, and he was the most beautiful, most behaved dog ever born. He was followed by Sparky whom I received from Aunt Ada. He was all white with long hair, and born on the Fourth of July, hence his name Sparky. As good as Asta was, Sparky was bad. Sparky and I'd be walking down the alley with some of my friends, and Sparky would bite one of their hands. He bit three times before, via court order, he was no longer allowed in the alley. When I went away to Frostburg, Sparky stayed behind, and Dad said he sent him to a farm where he could run free. Hmm.

Our row home had three bedrooms and one bathroom that contained a huge skylight on the top floor. On the main level, there was a living room with a built-in to the side of the stairs bookcase, a dining room, and a Pullman kitchen. From the kitchen, there was a stairway down to a full semi-finished basement with wood paneling and a green-tiled floor. There were zillions of front steps up to the house, not that we minded, because there was parking out back on the edge of the playground on the other side of the alley; and once we opened the gate to our backyard, after fifteen feet, there were only three steps to the back porch.

On the playground, there was a sliding board that was at least seven feet high with a sandbox to the right. Patrick, who was six feet one inch would lift Margot on the slide and let her slide down it. Scarier for me than for them, but that's what dad's do. They're not near as chicken as we mothers. However, here's the worst part: the slide was safer than the sandbox. Margot got worms, and the doctor said that was because the cats went to the bathroom in the sandbox. No more playing in that sandbox. We got one for our yard with a lid.

We had a cat named Smokey, so named because he was a smoky gray color. He appeared one day, stayed about six months, was gone, and would reappear in about six months. He did this for about four years, and then he was gone. We believed he lived with someone else in the neighborhood, but who's to say; he may have had a home in Florida.

We sold the '62 Chevy. Patrick decided that we could no longer afford two cars after we bought my dad's house in the city. I didn't want to sell it, but I wasn't working, and there was a bus only two blocks from our house. Other than the small hole in the middle of the back seat that you had to tell someone it was there or they wouldn't notice it, the car was pristine. Sometimes, though, you just have to give in, so we sold it.

I held a "tea" for Donald Schaffer, the democrat who was running for mayor of Baltimore City. He wanted to create what is now the showcase of Baltimore, the Inner Harbor, which at that time was an unremarkable waterfront. Mr. Schaffer didn't have a lot of love for teachers and was unresponsive to the folks who said that the poor could use that money better than putting it toward the Inner Harbor.

I had a date some years before with a guy who was a republican, and he took me to the republican meeting where he thought Barry Goldwater was going to win the presidency. He didn't win, but Gordo gave me the idea to register as a republican, which irritated my dad because he was a lifelong democrat. I loved my dad, but a daughter has to be an irritant now and then.

My dad was happy that I held a "tea" for Donald Schaffer, but Patrick was not happy with me. Actually, Donald Schaffer did not attend, but he sent Hyman Pressman, the City Comptroller. I had invited my neighbors and supplied them with lemonade and cookies. They asked Mr. Pressman questions, and after about an hour, the "tea" was done. Thank goodness, Patrick forgave me as soon as the "tea" was over.

The A&P

Our neighbor from across the street came to our house and asked if I
wanted to work for the Atlantic and Pacific Tea Company (A&P grocery store.) She worked there and had gotten several women jobs as
cashiers. It was a part-time job, and the schedules varied from week
to week, but that was okay because I didn't want to work full time.
The A&P paid very well, more than I had been earning as a waitress
for Howard Johnson's. I can remember my fingers being sore from
counting money after my first day of work. My neighbor had hired
so many cashiers that the manager called us Martha's girls. I don't
know why Martha asked me if I wanted the job, but I was surely
grateful she did.

We got a free dog named Clarence from one of my customers.
I thought his tail had a natural bend to it. Billy insisted through his
laughter that he must have been caught in a door. He was all white
except for his face, which was all black with a white stripe down to the
middle of his nose. Clarence liked to dig. Our row home had a small
yard, and after he got through digging, it looked like a minefield, so
he had to go. We put an ad in the paper, and a lady responded who
said she had a small farm and that he could dig to his heart's content.
He did all of his sit, lay down, paw kind of tricks for the lady, and she
took him, hopefully, to a wonderful home where he could just dig.

After our wedding, my brother Billy had enlisted in the Army
for the Vietnam War, and when he returned home, he lived with us
for a little over a year in the city. He and Patrick got along great. Billy
and Frank had been friends as well as brothers, and they thought of
Patrick as one of them. On Christmas Eve, Billy and Patrick spent
the night drinking beers, walking to the drug store in the Westview
Shopping Center—a mile or two from our home—and doing their

shopping. They made several trips. They wrapped the presents—sort of—and enjoyed themselves thoroughly.

All our married lives, Patrick and Billy were friends. Patrick and I were sad when Billy moved out. I was pregnant with our son. Billy had been dating Julie for a quite a few months. He was ready to have his own family, so he married Julie. They're still married and today, have two children, Jonathan and Mark; their wives, Emily and Morgan; and three grandchildren: Roy, Eve, and Joseph.

Our Youngest Baby

On November 26, 1971, Lance was born. We came home with a doll for Margot from her new brother. She was unimpressed, but we did find a use for the dump truck Santa had given her last Christmas because the doll needed a ride.

Lance was named for my cousin, Lance Gull. I always wanted to name my children for someone whom I hoped they would be like. Uncle Edwin took us to visit our cousin's family in the summer, Lance was always nice to Sarah and me. His mom probably told him to be nice to us. He was around thirteen years old and stuck with two young girls for a couple of hours, but he was always kind; played hide and seek, tag, and catch; and talked nice to us in their living room until it was time for us to leave. We went to visit his family every summer until I was eleven. Every now and then, I would hear about our summer relatives. I heard Lance had done well, becoming a scientist, mating gnat's eyes. Yeah, I don't know why he mated gnat's eyes; but being a scientist is a good job, gnats or no gnats.

Lance was the best kind of baby. Ten, two, and six were when he woke up, got changed, and went back to sleep. But I was used to Margot, who woke up when she felt like it, got changed, and stayed up a while. I had to learn to be on a schedule. And I kind of think Margot got her unscheduled ways from her mother.

At Christmastime, Margot had asked Santa for a bike. I wanted her to have one, but I just didn't have the money to buy one. I looked everywhere at every store, but I couldn't find one I could afford. So I looked in the newspaper. I found exactly the bike she wanted. It was orange with a black banana seat. It was fully assembled, and there wasn't a scratch on it. It looked brand new. It cost $25. I could afford that. Patrick was happy that he didn't have to assemble it, and I was happy that we didn't have to listen to him assemble it with his array of colorful words. On Christmas Day, Margot was happy to get from Santa just what she'd asked for, and her mother was happier than she was.

The A&P was a fun place to work, primarily because the customers were friendly. Some of them made me doilies, and lots of them bagged their own groceries. Not only did I get a dog from them, but a few months later, another customer asked if I wanted a kitten. I went to her apartment and the cutest kitten in the world mewed at me, so I brought her home. The children loved her right away, and you could tell that she loved us because she smiled as only kittens can do. She had calico markings on her face near her right ear. She had big brown eyes, and she was gentle and loving. She was so little that we named her Peanut. She grew to be a regular-sized cat, but still on the small size. Most of the time, she slept with Lance at night. As she grew, Lance would write on her with magic marker, mainly on her arms—good thing her fur was mostly white. She never seemed to mind. In fact, I believe she enjoyed it. She also enjoyed being outdoors. We bought a jeweled green collar which we attached to a dog-run leash. (I'm sure you've seen one of them, usually attached to a clothesline.) We attached it to a stake in the ground by the front porch. So when we were outside, she was too. She liked to hop on the hood of our car parked in the driveway, and she liked to greet everyone with a scowl and a meow. After all, she was our watch kitten.

Going to the Dogs

When the children were two years and five years old, we were at the mall, looking at the pet shop. The children were playing with a puppy, and you could see that the puppy liked them. It's weird how you never actually pick out a pet. They pretty much pick you out. We bought the brindle (red) Cairn Terrier and named her Muppet. She was the only dog we've ever purchased from a dealer. All the rest have been rescues, except Sher whom we bought from a breeder. Muppet only lived about four years before she got diabetes. The doctor said she wouldn't make it home, so I let him put her down. I thought my heart would break. And then I had to go home and tell the rest of my family.

There was an ad in the paper for a dog named Missy. I called and went to see the dog who was really fat, but I was a little pudgy, too. I liked her, so I brought her home. She had black curly hair, sort of like a cocker spaniel. Everything was okay for a few days, but one early morning, I woke up to some noise under the bed. I poked Patrick and told him, so he had to get out of the bed and look under it. "Oh no," said he. "That dog is having puppies under our bed." It took a couple of hours, but Missy cleaned up as her babies were born. There were six of them. They all looked cute, just like Missy.

We had an Aunt Ada who was married to Uncle Billy—Billy's name sake. She was a true animal lover. She actually left her one-million-dollar estate to one of the animal charities. I believe she was unhappy that I hadn't checked out the lady with the farm for Clarence. She told me not to worry, that she would take care of finding good homes for the puppies, and she did. She interviewed each person who inquired about taking a puppy. She said you had to charge some money to insure that the puppies would be in a good home. She gave the puppy money to an animal charity. Yea, Aunt Ada! Here's the weird part though. A few months after Missy gave birth, she was gone, so we looked everywhere. We found her in a neighbor's yard two blocks away from our home. I opened the gate, and Missy came running. Well, once I got her home, she went to the bathroom all over the house, and that night she cried to go out. I put her in the yard, and when I went to get her, she was gone. I walked down the two blocks and there she was in their yard, and the gate was locked. She looked happy and didn't come to me, so I left her there. It must be true that animals can pick you, and they can unpick you. I would check on her now and then, and she seemed okay, so that's where she lived.

We got a puppy from the newspaper we named Gendarme— French, or so we thought—for police. I took him for a walk without a leash. The girl who ran over him cried as much, if not more than me. You would think I would have learned from Asta that you can lose your dog if you don't keep a constant eye on them, or at least keep them on a leash. Our children cried for three nights.

Hope He Didn't Know

After we were married about eight years, Patrick asked his dad for a loan. It had something to do with the car, but I'm not sure why we needed the money. His dad said that his money was tied up and that it would really be a hassle to get it. Patrick told his dad that that was okay. Patrick made a loan at the credit union, which if he had thought of it, he probably would have done instead of asking his dad.

All those years I never thought much about Patrick's request, until the other night when my sister-in-law told me how my father-in-law used to send Marty and her money many times a year. She said they'd receive a note from Patrick's dad addressed to Tom, their firstborn, many times a year with money inside. His dad wrote Tom that he should give the money to his parents for the gas and electric bill or for food, or for whatever. I don't think Patrick knew that. I hope he didn't.

Moving to the County

After five years, we moved from the city to the county because we could not get Margot to school easily. There was no transportation. Patrick and I were working. You could walk to the Baltimore County School from our house. Patrick was teaching in the county, but tough beans, he couldn't get her in the county school system. So we moved to a county. We saw a realtor, drew a circle around Baltimore City on the map, said we needed walking distance from a school, and asked him to find us a place. He did. An almost new semi-detached in Anne Arundel County. We bought it. It had a nice, partially fenced big yard. Patrick and his Dad put up the rest of the fence.

A neighbor was getting rid of their aboveground pool, so we took it. Patrick put it up and built a deck on the side. It was very nice. The thing was that there was a large tree in the yard, so the pool water was always cold. However, when you have a pool, you invite friends to come, and they invite you to their warm pool. Our neighbors were great. We played cards every Sunday night with Addie and Korey across the street. One year, during the snowstorm, Patrick and Korey got two neighbors to help them lift our Volkswagen over the snowdrift in front of our driveway, and the four of us rode to the grocery store which was pretty much empty, but it was open. But still, the house was attached to another house. I had grown up in row houses, and I wanted to live in a single house.

This area had been mostly family beach properties where most of its residents only lived here in the summer. Now times were changing, and more people lived here full time. The residents who had lived here previously didn't like the change. It was a hard place to fit in. After we bought our house, we looked for a church. There was a tiny one at the top of our neighborhood, but Patrick nixed that one. "Too small," said he. "They'll be looking at us." So we went to the next one which was where we stayed. Armiger United Methodist Church had just moved a few years before when they expanded. They called it the friendly church, and they were, after the service. But when Lucy, who was new to the church too, and I tried to join the women's society, the ladies told us we could join if we started our own group in the society. That didn't make us feel very welcome.

Learning to Swim

Because Riviera Beach had water access, I felt it was imperative that our children learned to swim. We had a pool, and Margot jumped in and swam like a fish, but I could not get Lance to even put his face in the water. That summer, the Red Cross offered swimming lessons for two weeks in Rock Creek, and I signed them up. I can still see Lance standing in the creek in front of the pretty teenage instructor who told Lance to put his face in the water. He did it, just like that. It wasn't long before they both swam like fish.

The Most Out-of-This-World Accident

One of the best things about living in Riviera Beach was that it was off the main road, which meant that almost all of the traffic was local, so we felt fairly safe riding our bikes in the community. Margot, Lance, and I liked to ride around the beach two or three times, or more, a week.

Margot had a cobalt-blue racing bike, and Lance had a red racing bike. I had a 1950's blue/green with a rear fender bike. They had all kinds of gears and hand brakes, and Margot's had streamers. I was glad they had the kind of bikes they wanted, but I was more glad to have my bike that stopped when I put my feet on the pedals. Contrary to popular belief, my bike went just as fast as theirs did.

One day, I was rounding the corner on Virginia Avenue, near Saint Jane Frances Church, when I saw Lance to my left and an oncoming biker coming head on to Lance. It was surreal. I didn't think to yell or scream to let them know they were going to collide. I just watched them hit head on. Thank goodness they weren't hurt; just scratched up a little.

Kindergarten

When we entered Lance in kindergarten, I volunteered to help on Friday afternoons. While I had more fun than the law allowed, I also learned something valuable to me. After a week or so, we were in a circle and were picking the children to play in an activity. The teacher said to me that it was okay for me to pick Lance. I realized that I never favored my children in a group. I didn't want to show favoritism. After that day, I tried my hardest to include my own children and to show them a little extra favor.

The Circus

Where the Lauer's Super Thrift grocery store, the M&T Bank, the Rite Aid, and a few smaller stores sit today at the front of Riviera Beach, it used to be a huge vacant lot which was where the circus set up their tent. It was a small circus, but you could walk to it from our house; and when the children had to use the restroom, we just walked home and back again. There weren't any animals; but there were clowns, face painting, and high-wire acts. Margot and particularly Lance were impressed because there were even motorcycles that rode on the high wires. Probably because of this initial circus we had attended, every year, we attended small circuses which occurred in neighborhoods across the counties. After we had grandbabies, we took them also to the circuses.

Three years ago, my youngest granddaughter, Libby, and I rode an elephant. He hardly had any hair, and what he had was like wire. Last year, we each rode on a one-hump camel. It sort of felt like riding on a small horse. Twice, we attended the Barnum and Bailey Circus at the Civic Center in Baltimore City; and while that was exciting and fun, so were all of the smaller circuses.

Staying in the County

When Margot was eight years old and Lance five years old, we actually thought about moving to Missouri. I had corresponded with Patrick's granddad, Brad, no middle initial, Wightisle, since we first married. He'd retired to California where the bulk of his six children lived. He no longer lived in Braymer, Missouri, but I still felt like it might be a good place to raise our children. I know everyone says they escaped from little towns, but it sounded good to me. Patrick applied for a teaching position, and we drove on a trip to Missouri. They offered him the job with one stipulation, that he shave his mustache. None of the teachers were allowed to wear facial hair. When we returned home, Patrick called the Missouri Board of Education and declined the job.

While we were on the trip to Missouri, we spent a night at a hotel where Margot fell out of bed, hitting her head on the nightstand on her way to the floor. I called the front desk, and they brought a courtesy van which whisked Margot and I away to the hospital where the doctor sewed two stitches in her left eyebrow where she still carries the tiniest of scars. When we returned to the hotel, Patrick and Lance were still asleep. When we returned home, I sent the hotel a letter of thanks. What could have been an awful experience became easy, thanks to the hotel staff.

While I'm thinking about great-granddad, I'm reminded of his great claim to fame. He lived to be ninety-seven years old, and in all of that time, he did wonderful things: married, raised a family, became the president of the local bank, and welcomed me to the Wightisle family via a letter sent to Patrick's parents. But his claim to fame was that in his early twenties, he was working in a bank as a teller when it was robbed by Jessie James.

Birthdays

Margot was born on November 27, 1968, the day before Thanksgiving. Lance was born on November 26, 1971, the day after Thanksgiving. Lance was induced, so I could have had him on Margot's birthday, but I decided that everyone should have their own day.

When Margot and Lance were little, we traveled to both Patrick's parents and to Dad and Henrietta's for Thanksgiving. We celebrated at both houses Margot's birthday, and then Margot and Lance's birthdays. After Dad and Henrietta moved to Florida, we traveled only to Patrick's parents' house and celebrated their birthdays there. Of course, Dad and Henrietta called them on their respective birthdays and presents came in the mail.

Patrick's mother always baked a Wightisle birthday cake. It was a decadent chocolate cake with cinnamon and other secret ingredients. It was the best cake I have ever eaten. His mom always put silver dollars in the bottom of the cake, and when his dad cut the cake, the children would each get money in their piece. That was always fun for them.

As they got older, we'd have other birthday parties in addition to Thanksgiving. One of their most fun parties was at Pops, an Italian-themed restaurant. We had two tables, one at each end of the restaurant, so they sort of had separate parties. They and their friends celebrated with pizza and other foods and drinks, and Margot and Lance each had their own cake. Everyone was impressed with the red Pops balloons that came with paper feet, so it could "stand" on its own, that they got to take home.

One year, I made a huge mistake. I ordered Margot and Lance one whole sheet cake with both their names on it. It was an at-home party, and I got a lot of pitiful looks from both our children and their friends. I never made that mistake again. That was their only shared cake.

As our children became adults and married, we had parties for their spouses too. Because Samantha's birthday is in December, we celebrated her birthday with Margot and Lance on Thanksgiving Day. After dinner, Lance, Samantha, and their girls came to my house after dinner with Samantha's family. Margot and Luke went to dinner with us, so they would already be there. We would have three ice cream cakes with candles, and we would sing. They would then open their gifts. Luke's birthday is on February 22, so we would wait until then to celebrate his birthday by everyone going to dinner at a restaurant.

For Patrick's sixtieth birthday, I threw him a surprise party. We always decorated our house for every occasion, including birthdays, and he didn't notice the extra bowls of snacks, etc. I invited tons of people who all came. Billy asked me if we were going to yell "happy birthday." "No." They just all came around the same time. As each person entered the house, they wished Patrick a happy birthday.

After a bit, Patrick said, "Hey, babe, is this a birthday party for me?"

I grinned and said, "Surprise. Happy birthday."

Schramm's

Schramm's Farm was a great place—not big, just fun. They had a small area where they sold produce. For Halloween, they had a huge cardboard pumpkin figure with a hole for its mouth where the children could reach in and bring out a lunch-sized bag of candy and assorted plastic toys.

Schramm's was a ten-minute ride from our house. Most Christmases, we went tree shopping at Schramm's Farm. They had acres of trees, all sizes, all kinds. I worked almost every Saturday, so we usually went early and picked out our tree. But this one Saturday, we couldn't find a tree, and I didn't want to be late for work, so Patrick and our children were left to pick out the tree. When I got home that evening, there was a five-foot tall bush in our living room in the tree stand. There appeared to be four or five stems taller than the rest, so we put the star on the one closest to the middle. We decorated the bush, pardon me—tree, while we sang Christmas carols, just like every other year. I made sure that every year after that, I had time to help pick out the tree.

Hanging Out with Family

Through the years, we would go out with Billy and Julie. Sometimes, we'd visit them at their house for karaoke at Christmas time; every July Fourth, they'd have a cookout—stuff like that. But most of the time, we'd go somewhere. For a while, we took polka dance lessons at Julie's Russian Catholic Church. We learned to polka, and while we weren't the best, Patrick and I had fun dancing the polka. Another time, we learned to disco dance. We actually were pretty good at the disco dance. Patrick and I would attend parties where we didn't know too many people there so we could practice our dancing. For us, the disco dancing was kind of wild fun.

When Margot was ten years old, she fell off a bicycle, and the pedal caught her leg. The doctor at our hospital sewed her leg, wrapped it, and in a few weeks, it healed. We went to a pool party a day or two after it was healed. She jumped in the air during a volley-ball game and came down to an open wound. I'm sure I should have known that she should be careful, but I'm not always as smart as I should be. Our friend, Ryan, was there—Mr. MacGyver, as named by Lance. He fixed her well enough to return to the hospital. This time, it took a lot longer to heal and left her with a faint scar, but she doesn't have any ill effects from it. At forty-six years old, the scar is almost invisible; and as part of her exercise routine, she runs almost every day.

Trips to Florida

After Dad and Henrietta moved to Florida, Patrick, Margot, Lance, and I would drive to Florida for a week in the winter. I was always worried that we would mess up their routine when we came. I didn't realize how much our visiting mattered to my dad. One time, when we were leaving to come home, I had forgotten something. We had only been gone ten minutes or so. When we returned, I found my dad crying on the screened porch. I asked if he was okay. He said he was just a little melancholic because we'd left.

Sometimes, Margot, Lance, and I would fly to Florida for a few days in the winter. It was wonderful to see Dad and Henrietta for more than one week in the winter. On one of those occasions, my dad and Lance found a snake in his garden, and Dad and Lance killed the snake and burned it in the fire pit. For years, they talked about how exciting that was.

Church Stuff

After about a month of attending Armiger United Methodist Church, Patrick and I started teaching Sunday school. They needed the teachers. He had the high school class. He was always good with teaching. He had a knack for it, although he always understated his abilities. He taught all week, and most teachers I've met needed a two-day rest each week, so he found something he liked to do, even better than teaching, and that was counting money. Todd was the head money counter at that time. You couldn't talk when they were counting, and he was pretty stern. I knew this because now and then, they would be short a money counter, and Patrick would take me down there to help them. I was no money counter. I liked teaching Sunday school, and I had the best grade, which was third grade. At that age, they could read and weren't mischievous yet. Because I helped fairly regularly. I was sort of good at counting, but it wasn't my cup of tea.

Patrick stopped teaching Sunday school, but he became a mentor to the students joining the church. Most, if not all of the mentors, took their students out regularly. Most of the time, they went to fast-food places—which were the new and upcoming business at that time—and talked about the homework and whatever else they wanted. Years later, one of Patrick's mentored students came to see him after church when he was in the power chair. Jeff talked to him a long time, thanking him for being a great mentor. That meant a lot to Patrick.

When Margot was twelve years old, I decided it was time for her to attend the church youth group. I had a wonderful friend, Judy, who was in her eighties, but you'd never know it because she was, as they say, young at heart; and she was still in great shape, health-wise. She encouraged me to attend that year's first youth group meeting.

The preacher was sitting at his desk. A "couple" were sitting together in the chair next to the preacher. One boy, Margot, and I were sitting on the wooden sofa; and Judy was sitting on the chair next to the wooden sofa. After the meeting, Judy said, "Now you know why I wanted you to come."

For the next nine years, I volunteered to be the youth leader; and until she died, Judy was the co-youth leader for seven years. When Lance turned twelve years old, he and his friends also joined the youth group. We held lock-ins, which were when the children stayed overnight, but were not allowed to sleep, eat, or drink anything but water. We fed them breakfast in the morning, and people paid money to the lock-in for every hour the child they sponsored stayed awake. At the lock-in, Judy always brought her individual trampoline. She would walk on it during the night. The children, and I, were very impressed.

We usually had around twenty-five children participating, so we made a considerable amount of money. We had a child whose brother had died from cancer, and we gave the lock-in money to the Cancer Society. We went to Camp Manidokan for a Bible study retreat/fun week once a year. We sang Christmas carols to the elderly at the nursing home and to the shut-ins still in their homes. Every week, we met on Sunday nights with the preacher and discussed issues of the day. We were busy and we had lots of fun.

Ocean City Vacations

The children and I vacationed most years in Ocean City, camping at the Ocean City Frontier Town Camp Ground with Billy and Julie. We had a huge pink tent with a sleeping area in the back and a screened living area in the front. After we'd spend the day in Ocean City, getting our pictures taken in old-time clothes, walking and riding bikes on the boardwalk, swimming in the ocean, and eating all kinds of fudge and french fries, etc., we'd return to the campground to have dinner and hang out with Billy and Julie and their boys, Jonathan and Mark. There was a pool with ocean salt water in it. There was a stagecoach trip around the campground where you were "robbed" by a gun-toting robber. All of our children slept very well at night. I guess they were exhausted.

After the children went to sleep, Julie, Billy, and I sat in their tent and enjoyed playing cards.

Most of the years, Patrick stayed home. He'd put the tent on top of the car so it wouldn't blow off, and he'd make sure everything was A-OK with the car. One year, on the way home, the tent fell off the car. I wasn't as adept as Patrick in tying down the tent. The couple of times he went with us, he'd wait in the car until we set up the tent. One year, it rained and rained and rained, so we—Lance, Margot, and I—set the tent up in the rain. Patrick complained and complained, and complained. Then he said, "Let's go have dinner." After we had dinner on the boardwalk, we all felt better. Then we came back to the campground and went to sleep. The sun came out the next day. We went back into Ocean City and enjoyed walking the boardwalk and eating french fries and other assorted junk foods. Life was good again.

One year, Suzanne went with Lance, Harry (Lance's friend), and me for vacation. Margot had a softball tournament, so she couldn't attend. We set up the tent as usual, but we weren't careful, and we had a tree root in the sleeping area. Ouch. Then when we returned from the ocean, we found that the birds had eaten our food. Thank goodness for Julie because she fed us hotdogs and other stuff. On the way home, in those days, you had to pay a toll both ways at the bridge, but I had spent all the money I'd brought. We didn't use cards, just money, so I didn't have any money for the toll. I had to borrow money from Suzanne to pay the toll. I repaid her as soon as we returned home, but I did feel like a heel when I had to borrow her money.

We Needed a Ride

We kept the Volkswagen for ten years. In the end, it just died, so Patrick gave it to his youngest brother who liked to work on cars. It was Patrick's intent that Marty would keep the car, but after he souped it up, he gave it back to us. You didn't have to put your foot on the gas pedal, you just had to turn on the key and the bug would start moving, kind of fast. He had taken out the radio, and it was really cold what with the air coming through the radio opening. We finally gave it to a teenager in our neighborhood.

So we needed another car, and we didn't have a lot of money to spend on one, so we looked in the newspaper and found a used Chevy Vega. It was orange, and for the first four years, it ran well. But the last year, it started to burn oil; and it seemed that every day, it burned more oil. In the end, a policeman gave me a ticket to have the car repaired or at the very least, removed from the road. It would have cost more to have the car repaired than it was worth, so I looked for another vehicle.

I found a brand-new white truck at the Chevy dealer in Edmondson Village. I had never been in there before. It looked like every other automobile showroom. There was no sign that a deer had run into their glass-fronted showroom. Nothing. Anyway, I bought a truck. I went to the credit union to get a loan. They gave it to me, but have you ever had the sickening feeling that you shouldn't do something you're about to do? Well, sitting there, getting ready to sign the papers, I realized that this was more money than I wanted to spend. Patrick seemed okay with getting the truck loan, but he never liked to spend money and particularly borrowed money. So when I said I was going to return the truck, he didn't have much to say. I believe he was disappointed, but he never complained to me about not getting the truck. In those days, there was no "three-day you can change your mind" kind of contract. It was a hard thing to return a vehicle. The salesman didn't want to accept it. He told me to leave it on the street if I didn't want it. I had to eat a lot of crow, but he finally agreed to put it in their shop and to cancel the contract. I got it done. I followed my gut. Hopefully, that was the right thing to do. For a while, we made do with one car. But I was working at the grocery store, and we needed another vehicle.

We bought a brand-new Chevy Chevette. It was almost the light, zenith-blue color of our Volkswagen. Now that I look back on it, we bought a lot of blue vehicles. We kept that car a long time, longer than we probably should have. The first six or seven years, it ran great. Then as it aged, it had problems. The floor on the driver's side rusted out. Patrick and the children found a metal sign in the woods which they used to cover the floor. The children always teased Patrick that he owned the Fred Flintstone mobile. If you recall, Fred used his feet to stop his car. When it was around ten years old, we finally gave it to one of Lance's friends.

School

When Margot was in the first grade, I tried to help with her first homework assignment. I yelled at her because she wasn't getting it done as quickly and efficiently as I thought she should. I decided that day that I was a lousy homework helper, and let her and her brother do their homework on their own time. I figured if they didn't do it, the teacher would let me know. This system worked well for eight years. But when Margot was in middle school, she had a terrible time when taking her algebra math classes, so we had to get a new system. Patrick tried to help her with pre-algebra, but she wasn't "getting it," and she wasn't receptive to his helping her. So as the inexperienced parents of a teenager, we punished her. She had to study in her room for fifteen minutes each evening in the first quarter. In the second and third quarters, we bumped up her punishment to half an hour. Had we given her punishment more thought, we would have made her study near us. She loved going to her room. She read *Charlotte's Web* at least sixteen times, and all of her dolls "lived" in her room. My mother would have loved playing dolls with her. Even when she was older, she didn't mind being in her room. At the beginning of the fourth quarter, I was finished with phone calls and notes. I made an appointment to speak directly with her teacher. At that meeting, her teacher complained that Margot was unresponsive to him and that she didn't complete her class work. He went to get a sample of Margot's work. When he left the room, another teacher who was grading papers in the cafeteria where we met, told me that I should listen to my daughter. When Margot's teacher returned, I thanked him for the meeting and left. When we got outside, I told Margot that her punishments were over. Patrick and I hired a tutor who said that it was too late to teach her anything except some algebra math tricks, which he used to helped her pass the class.

Here's the surprise. Margot had decided that she wasn't good in math in middle school and in high school, but decided to try to work with numbers when she was attending college and found out that she was good at it. She now holds a Master of Business Administration, also known as lots of math.

Patrick was good at teaching. He didn't mind that he had to buy supplies for the students twice a year. Generally, he was tight with his money, but he wanted his students to do well. He believed that repetition was a huge part of teaching. Yeah, you could make it as fun as you could, but the bottom line—at least to him—was that repetition was the key to learning. Some of his superiors didn't agree. They believed that you had to make the students want to learn and that was the teacher's job. The only thing that saved Patrick was that his students tested well. Testing is everything. They still test students today, and the tests are still very important to the teacher's annual review.

One time, our youngest, Lance, came home from school with a certificate saying that he knew his times tables. When we sat that evening at the dinner table, we were waiting for him to regale us with his newfound knowledge. Oh yes, he knew his times tables, if you stayed in order: 4x3=12, 4x4=16; but if they got out of order, he was lost. So for the next few weeks, we "played" times tables for fun at dinner. I didn't know how much fun the children had tossing times tables back and forth to each other and to Patrick and I, but everyone in our house knew their times tables.

After we'd been married for ten years, Patrick decided he'd had spent enough time as a teacher. One of the parents came to school and told him that her daughter had too much homework and therefore, had trouble attending her dance classes. That was the straw that broke the camel's back. He resigned that day. He got a job as an insurance salesman, but he only sold two policies in six months. Then he got a job scrubbing floors, but it wasn't a constant job with a regular paycheck. He was fortunate enough to get a job as a mailman, but that only lasted through the summer. Then he became a guard on an armored truck and then a night watchman for a factory. After that, he got a job as manager of a bowling alley. He liked that and worked there for over a year. But it didn't pay much, and the hours were long, so he took a job as a social worker. Finally, he decided that he had wanted to be a minister before I'd met him at Frostburg. So in September, three years after he left teaching, he walked out the door in the morning and told me that when he returned, he'd either be going to the seminary for ministry, keeping the job as a social worker, or going back to teaching. He returned home as a teacher. I don't know why he picked teaching, and I didn't think he knew why either. You know that old saying, "You go with the devil you know," rather than trying out an uncertainty.

Patrick spent the next ten years in Baltimore City before he retired and got a job that he loved doing at The Widgets Testing Agency, Inc. He was starting to have trouble standing for any length of time, and you need to be able to stand in elementary school as a teacher. As hard as it was for him physically in the City, his time at The Widgets Testing Agency, Inc. was pleasurable because he could sit at his desk doing his job as a paralegal proofreader, and he only dealt with other employees in work-related discussions or in social settings.

Single House

We moved from the semi-detached house to a single, white-with-black-shutters, four-level split on Sandy Beach Drive. What a chore. First, Patrick had to be persuaded to move. He never liked change, and moving was a huge change. We moved less than a mile away, and even though it was the same school district, no one was happy, except me. I wanted a single-family dwelling, and this was it.

Periodically, we would update our children's bedrooms. Margot started out with the Flintstones. When she was a pre-teenager, her room had yellow walls. She had curtains, a bedspread, and a rug that all matched with yellow roses on a white background. After we moved to Sandy Beach Drive, Margot started to do the updating on her own room. She paid for and installed everything in her room. She had some sort of geometric pattern, then a purple room, and then a pink room with the closet wallpapered in a blue flowered pattern.

Lance's rooms started with Spiderman. Next, he had a blue room, and the last two room makeovers were baseball and then football themed. My youngest granddaughter Libby inherited Lance's bedroom when we swapped houses. I would smile when I hung up Libby's sweater or other clothing item when I tucked her in bed on Wednesday evenings because I would notice Lance's football wallpaper boarder on top of the baseboard in her closet. Yes, we put the border on the top of the bottom baseboard as well as at the ceiling.

We were two houses from the creek, boat ramp, and playground. The school buses came every morning. The neighbors were friendly. I joined the association and therefore, got to do all kinds of fun stuff. I was Mrs. Clause a few years. Although I will tell you that after Santa walks into their house, Mrs. Clause is unnecessary, except for bringing in the gifts from outside that the parents put out for Santa to give to the children. I got to help with a few Easter egg hunts, summer association parties at the playground, and other assorted fun stuff. We were invited to Halloween parties and yard parties, and on and on. Plus, we were close enough that we still were friends with our neighbors from our previous neighborhood. All good.

The only problem was that I got laid off by the A&P Grocery Store right after we bought the house. Finding a job was difficult at best. I would go to the places of business and the people would try to hide their nameplates because in those days, jobs were scarce. You had to physically go to the businesses to apply for the jobs, and you had to write down the name of the person with whom you spoke. No one seemed to want to be involved. I guess they had a job and didn't want to be involved with someone laid-off. I finally got a job with Montgomery Wards, working in the bargain center. I went from $10.26 an hour to $3.35 an hour. Thank goodness I was not the sole income for my family. I would have had to get a second or third job.

Many times in life, a particular person will make a huge difference; and at the time, you don't even notice. The Widgets Testing Agency, Inc. called me at work at Montgomery Wards to offer me a job. I had applied for a job listed in the newspaper. You had to pass a typing test of forty words per minute, and a written test with English and math. I did that, but hadn't heard anything from them. When the man called, I told him I couldn't take the job because I needed to give two weeks' notice. They wanted me there the following Monday. Ruth, my manager, asked me to ask the caller to hold on just a moment. I did. And then she said to me, "You have two weeks vacation time. Take it. We'll know that you're trying out the job and that you probably won't be back, but we'll be glad to see you if you don't like it there. And you can count your vacation time as two weeks' notice." So the main office didn't know it, but my boss did. I enjoyed working at The Widgets, so I accepted the job. Montgomery Wards never held a grudge because I still worked there for the Christmas holidays. Some years later, Montgomery Wards went out of business, but I still had a job, thanks to Ruth.

Widgets

The Widgets Testing Agency Inc. headquarters was located in Washington D.C. They tested all kinds of products for companies. Window companies used The Widgets for their claims that their windows were the best. One time, I brought a roast home after The Widgets held testing on various stoves. Patrick and the children loved that because they didn't think their wife and mother was much of a cook, and they enjoyed eating a deliciously cooked food.

In 1965, when I was a senior at Edmondson High School, I received the Betty Crocker Homemaker of the Year Award. It held no monetary value, but I was thrilled when I received the certificate at a ceremony in the auditorium. My home economics teacher had nominated me. I was a good seamstress and could bake a cake from scratch that would melt in your mouth. I didn't know how to cook a hotdog, but I was adept at many fancy dishes. You would think that I was a good cook, but you would be wrong. I've always had a problem with my weight. I attended several weight loss places over the years. There was one recipe that I particularly liked—lasagna with string green beans instead of pasta. It really tasted good, but our children could not get over the string green beans. Margot, to this day, eats green beans, but not string green beans. Not only was I chunky, but I also worked, and I always tried to cook in the most efficient manner. I liked the food to taste good, but I didn't care about the presentation. They would comment about my chicken noodle soup with the bones left in it. I would say that sucking the stock off a bone was delicious even if it was in the final product. My children didn't agree. I should have been embarrassed because our children would rather, on any given day, have had their dad's Hamburger Helper dinner. He'd open up a package of Hamburger Helper, brown some ground beef, throw in a couple cans of vegetables, and cook it in a pot on top of the stove. Everyone got a slice of bread, a drink, and they were good to enjoy dinner. I guess it was good that I worked, fixed dinner for the week on my nights off, and didn't fix dinner for every night.

One thing that I loved to do was to sew. I sewed mother-daughter dresses for Easter and was very happy with the products. Margot and I looked totally cool in our yellow dresses. All good things came to an end because when I lost my job at the A&P and after a few months got a job with Montgomery Wards in their bargain center, I learned that I could buy our clothes lots cheaper than I could make them. After that, my sewing skills were only used for crafts and repairs.

While I was working for The Widgets Testing Agency, Inc., Tom Clancy came to the Fort Meade Post Exchange (PX) for a book signing. He and a military guy had written a book, and they were going to be there. I waited in line for a few hours. I had taken a few vacation hours, and I told my office I'd be back as soon as I got my book signed. My friend, Shelly, retired military, had clued me in to the "signing" and got me a one-day parking pass. When it was our turn, a lady came by with a sandwich and a drink for each one of the signers. She told me I would have to wait. Woohoo. I tried not to be a pest, and I don't believe I was, but I got to speak with Mr. Clancy. He told me that he only worked a few weeks a year, doing book signings, and that he really enjoyed being a writer. I was very impressed. He was nice to me, and he didn't have to be.

When the General Counsel for The Widgets Testing Agency, Inc. retired, I gave him that book for his gift. I got to enjoy speaking with Mr. Clancy, I got to brag about speaking to Mr. Clancy, I got to have the book on my bookshelf for a few years, and I got to give the book as a gift. I don't think it gets much better than that. If I remember correctly, I only paid $35 for the book. I got a lot of bang for my buck!

Sporting World versus Scouts World

While I had grown up in a household without sports, our children grew up in a sporting household. Patrick loved to play, watch, discuss, and make files of sporting games. He actually kept score of the baseball games with all of the activity like balls and strikes, etc. When our children were around four years old, their sporting knowledge began. They were both enrolled in T-ball. As they grew, their expertise increased. Patrick was Margot's softball coach, and while he did not coach her soccer games, he never missed a practice. Lance played baseball and football. Patrick not only helped coach Lance's football practices, but he also umpired the baseball games. When there were games on television, the three of them watched; and when there were games on the radio, they listened.

Patrick's love of sports was actually his downfall. He was not a talented player. He was average in every sport he played. Margot and Lance were good at playing sports. They weren't always the best players, but they were good players. Patrick tried to live vicariously through his children. When Margot was a junior in high school, she decided that she didn't want to play soccer any more. Her dad was beside himself in that he expected her to play. She did not play soccer in her junior or senior year.

For almost her entire junior year, Margot and her dad spoke to each other only when necessary. Finally, one morning, I told Patrick that he would say "good morning" to Margot, and I told Margot that she would say "good morning" to Patrick. That evening, I told them both to say "hi" when they saw each other. I'm sure they were tired of being distant from each other, and they loved one another because it wasn't long before they were speaking as before the soccer fight.

Patrick had a similar experience with Lance, because Lance decided he was not going to play football in his senior year. Most important to Patrick was that Lance would not be attending the sports dinner that all of the dads attended with their sons. Neither Lance nor Patrick attended the sports dinner. Patrick learned from his spat with Margot that distant speech doesn't work and continued to speak with Lance.

All parents make mistakes, even the really good ones. But the truth is that parents are the adults. It's hard to let your children grow up, especially when you think they're making the wrong decision, but they have to make their own way in life. We taught our children to be independent people, and sometimes that came back to haunt us when they didn't see an issue as we did. Sometimes you just had to agree to disagree.

Margot was also a Brownie Scout. I had been a Brownie Scout, a Girl Scout, and a Senior Scout. I wanted that for Margot, but the Girl Scout troops in our area were having problems with who controlled the money and who had the authority of the troop. After less than a year, the troop folded. Never again did I put her in another troop, which was too bad because for the motherless girl like I had been, the Girl Scouts were a Godsend. Mrs. Smith was the troop leader, and she responded to my dad's requests for girl child-rearing help. My troop had all kinds of girl health classes and other classes about things usually a mom talks about with her daughters. Of course, we also had handicrafts and philanthropy activities. I have always been grateful for the Girl Scouts and in particular, Mrs. Smith.

Margot used her defunct Brownie Scout troop time to read to my dad—Pop Pop. Dad spent his winters in Florida and his summers on the farm in Carroll County. He visited us in Pasadena, so in the summer, he spent his time listening to Margot read. Margot was slim and trim with big brown eyes, like Patrick's mom, but everything she did and said reminded me of my mom. She liked to play with Barbie dolls; she read all of the time she wasn't playing sports. I often wondered if my dad could sense my mom's personality in her.

It seemed that in our house, when our children were younger and the weather was rainy or too cold, we were always playing card games: Crazy Eights, Hearts, Rummy 500, and War. We played other card games, but those were our favorites. Now and then, we'd play Monopoly or some other board game, but mostly we played cards.

Lance was a Cub Scout. Ryan, our neighbor and good friend, was the local Cub Scout leader. Lance called him MacGyver because like the guy on the television show, he could fix or make anything. The scouts sang for the elderly and were available to help any group that needed a hand. They had numerous outdoor activities. They camped, they ran races, and they learned how to use an ax and a saw. They had the car derby where they made little wooden cars and then raced them down a six or seven-foot wooden racetrack. Some of the dad's helped the scouts make the cars, but Patrick was a stickler for Lance making his own racecar. I don't believe Lance ever won a race, but he enjoyed making and racing his car. He had that creative pride that Patrick wanted for him. When it was time to cross the bridge to Boy Scouts, Lance's sporting activities took too much of his time, and he did not become a Boy Scout.

The Bear

The lady up the street was selling a shepherd husky, whom we named Bear. He was one smart dog. We put him on Lance's bed the first night in a crate. Lance took him out in the morning. We discarded the crate. Bear had one "accident" in his whole life when he was four or five years old. I came home from work and found him hiding behind the sofa. He was sick, I believe, because he pooped in the living room. He never had another accident. Bear made friends with the Peanut. They used to lay at the top of the stairs together. And you could find them often sleeping together in front of the sofa and of course, at night, with Lance. That is a smart dog.

Bear's first summer, he shed so much that after he arose from lying down, it looked like he was still there because there was so much hair. I decided to get a grooming kit from the store. Oh my goodness, he cried, wailed, and ran every time I got out the kit with the shaver in it. I couldn't bear his misery, so I took him to the groomers. When we went to get him, he had a beautiful blue bow on the top of his head. We put him in our yard, and he hid. He tried to take off the bow. While this sounds like animal cruelty, we were okay with his wearing the bow; but finally, Lance took it off him. The next summer, we had Bear shaved again, only this time, he loved the blue bow. He pranced up and down the fence so everyone could see it, and he wouldn't let you touch the bow. He was quite impressed with himself. I believe the bow finally disintegrated.

Margot had a rabbit named Joy who lived in her bedroom for a few years. She took great care of her. Joy had a litter box. Her only bad habit was that she liked to chew on the electrical cords. We only had Bear a few months when one day, Margot opened her door to find Bear looking in. Joy had a heart attack and died behind the dresser. Margot, Lance, Patrick, and I buried Joy in our backyard and said a few words over her about what a good rabbit she'd been.

Then there was the year Frank and Alice, Suzanne, Billy and Julie, Jonathan, Mark, Margot, Lance, Harry, Patrick, and I went to Ocean City together. We rented a roundhouse on the bay side. The house itself was round, with all of the interior walls being round, sort of like our house in Florida. We had lots of fun. We sent Lance and Harry with Frank's family three days early because I had to work. When Patrick and I arrived, we couldn't find Lance and Harry because they had a boat and were out on the bay. Margot and Suzanne were on the boardwalk. They were all having fun. Frank would walk early every morning on the boardwalk. Everyone walked the boardwalk, played games, and rode the rides. We had our pictures taken at the old-time picture studio. We rode bikes one day and took the tram one day up and down the entire boardwalk. We swam in the ocean and ate at all of the nifty restaurants. We all had more fun than the law allowed. Frank, Alice, and Suzanne took Lance and Harry with them on the way home. Frank said that when he opened our door, the Bear almost bit him on the arm, but thank goodness, Bear missed.

Bear had a problem and unbeknown to us, his mother had the same problem, which was they might bite you if you weren't part of the immediate family. When Bear was little, he didn't bite in the conventional way; he would sort of chew on you. As Bear got older, he became worse. At first, he would sort of slide his teeth down your hand, so we took him to the vet, and the vet said it was probably the "Dog days of August." Bear hated mailmen. My brother, Billy, was a mailman. Normally, Bear loved him; but one day, Billy came to see me with his uniform on. Had he not be adept at flinging his bag to thwart off dogs, Bear would have bit him.

Well, we had always kept a good eye on Bear because he was over 100 pounds, and we wanted to make sure everyone was safe. Although I will say, our children were told that if Bear did not come to the door, don't go in. So Bear was a big safe part of our home. We had a huge yard—about a third of an acre—and we had him always on a clothesline leash even when he was a puppy. Patrick had installed the kind of fence you use for small gardens by attaching it to the chain-link fence and folding the garden fence in half, with the lower half buried in the ground. He had also installed a fence on top of the chain-link fence. However, when Bear was nine years old, he dug up the buried fence, having it stuck in his mouth while he dug under the chain-link fence. He came up on the other side of the chain-link fence and bit the neighborhood mailman on the top of his thigh. The top of his thigh was just about the height of an elementary school kid. We loved this dog; but Patrick, Margot, Lance, and I all knew we had to put him down. After the quarantine placed on him by the Post Office, we fed Bear his favorite breakfast sausage. We took him for a ride to his favorite places around Brooklyn Park, and then we took him to the veterinarian to have him put down. Patrick grabbed Bear off the table and said, "No one's killing my dog," and left. That next Friday, Lance and I took Bear directly to the veterinarian, said our goodbyes, and left.

Sherlock

I had asked the veterinarian what kind of dog was the most gentle dog in the world. He told me to get a beagle. He said to be sure that it was a real beagle and not a pocket beagle. He said they were smaller, their tails more down than up, and that they were pretty much mean. I thanked him. I went home, looked in the newspaper, found a breeder who lived in Arbutus, Maryland, and bought a pedigreed beagle.

Learning from Gendarmes, the next day after Bear died, I brought home the beagle puppy whom we named Sherlock. He wasn't like Snoopy. He was a tricolor beagle. He had large, round, sad-looking eyes, a brown head with a white strip that ran from the top of his head, past his eyes and that spread all around his muzzle and nose, except for the black bulb on the end of his nose. He had the black fur that looked like a saddle on his back and down the sides. He had the white paws, the white chest, and the white end of the tail. He had the long, but not as long as a basset hound ears, and that wonderful beagle howl. His shoulders and legs were white with black ticking (small round dots). He hardly ever got on the furniture, but he needed to learn what every puppy needed to learn.

We never could figure out if he was stupid or smart, but we did know he was stubborn. Beagles have a tendency to cower if they're punished, and we did not want a cowering dog. When he refused to do his "business" outside, Margot and I took him to dog training. She was the trainer, and I was along for the ride—and the laughs. At home, Margot would put Sherlock outside on the longest leash you've ever seen for one or two hours at a time. She would walk around the yard with him, trying to get him to do his "business." The dog trainer said that was the way to do it. Sher never went to the bathroom on that leash. He waited until they came in the house to go. While Sher loved Margot and had no fear of her, he was afraid of the trainer. The trainer told Margot to give her his leash so she could train him in the "circle" of dogs. The moment the trainer came over, Sher started to urinate, and he urinated the whole time the trainer was near him. The only thing Sherlock learned from the training sessions was to sit. Anytime you wanted to take his picture, he would sit for you. Anything else, good luck! Oh, he did learn to do his "business" outside. We bought a pet door, and after that, he never had an accident in our house. And the neighborhood children who all loved Sher could crawl into the house to play with him through his pet door.

Our friend, Jackie, lived across the street from a lady who only kept puppies for about a year and then got rid of them. Jackie called us to see if we wanted another beagle. Of course, we did. We paid the lady for her one-year-old dog, Molly, who was the most motherly, gentle beagle dog we've ever known. She looked like Sher in that she was a tricolor beagle. But she was not chubby, and her head, including her nose and muzzle, was all brown. She liked to lick every-one—human, animal, you name it—in the face. She liked to hop on the furniture. The bonus was she was house trained. She slept on the bed between Patrick and I. She was a great beggar. She'd lift up her upper right lip and let it quiver. Patrick could not resist her, so she always got a treat from him. Here's the best part. That Christmas, we received a card from the lady, addressed to our dog, signed, Mommy. I still have that card. She didn't have any children, and I always won-dered (sarcastically, of course) if she would have kept a baby longer than a year.

Sherlock, Molly, and Milo

Molly and Sher liked to play tug of war. Both were easygoing. Molly was quicker than Sher, but shared with Sher, like when she stole the roast off the table. Patrick pulled the roast from her mouth, and she tried to eat it as fast as she could, but she never once tried to bite or snap at Patrick. Sher got a few bites of roast that fell on the floor during Patrick and Molly's tussle.

We decided to mate Sher and Molly. Their puppies would have pedigrees. Oh my goodness, what a disaster. We had never done anything like this, and we hadn't researched it. How hard could this be? Well, we believe Sher was too fat by this time; and although he did his best to impregnate Molly, who was willing, he couldn't get it done. What was worse was that he couldn't get it down, and we were worried he would die, so we called the vet whom I believe may still be laughing.

Billy really liked Sher and said that if I ever came across another dog like him, he would like to have it. By now, I was working in an office. I told some of my coworkers about Billy and Sher. Well, Chuck told me about a beagle that was free online. I called the lady, and she invited me to come pick up the "beagle." I knew he had beagle somewhere in him, but I wasn't sure where. He was a nice dog, but he had lousy bathroom habits. However, I wasn't worried because Billy always kept his dogs outside. I took the dog whom the lady had named Milo. Julie said, when I called them, "What's wrong with him?" That was how Milo came to live with Sher, Molly, and us.

Milo and Sher fought over Molly, so we had Molly spayed. After that, the boys got along. We never got Milo trained. We finally took up the carpet and covered the hardwood floors with tons of shellac. Other than that, he was a good dog. The grandchildren loved him and dressed him up all the time. I have a picture of him on top of the television all dressed up, and you can actually see him smile. He was smart in that he knew a good deal when he got it.

About a year after Milo came to live with us, we got mice in the house. I called an exterminator. He assured me that the mouse-traps could not hurt a dog or a cat. About two weeks after he came, Sherlock had one in his mouth; and before I could get to him, he started to shake it. The next day, he was full of vim and vigor. The day after, he was sad and throwing up; and on the way to the vets, he had a heart attack and died. Molly and Milo were as sad as we humans were. They looked for him for a few days, and then, I believe, they knew he wasn't coming home.

Sandwich Generation

We heard this story from Patrick's mom. She said that in World War II, she had a soldier boyfriend whom she was to marry, but he was killed in the war. Along came Patrick's dad who impregnated her. She said that he went home to his family to see how they felt about his situation. They told him to go back and marry Patrick's mother. He did. They were married for fifty-two years before Patrick's dad died.

Patrick's dad died in 1995, leaving his mother unable to cope with taking care of herself, business-wise. She could write a check, but either did not care to or could not learn how to write a check to pay bills. Patrick loved his mother and was not going to let her down. He was the oldest and felt it was his responsibility to care for his mother, and he did so for the next twenty years until he died. He went to visit her on Tuesday, every week. For the first fifteen years, he went alone, took care of the bills and any other business she needed done, and then he took her to dinner. He never missed a week, although he did have to change the day a few times. The next five years, he saw his mother every week, almost always on Tuesday. He could no longer drive to her house by himself, and after a while, he could no longer drive. So like any good son, he engaged his wife to give him a ride; and of course, I went to dinner too. He brought all of his mother's records, bills, etc. to our house; and he still went every week to dinner with his mother and me. Rain and snow had nothing to do with his not attending. We'd just have to go another day. Every week, Patrick's mom picked a restaurant, and we'd go there for dinner. One of our favorites was the Hunan restaurant in Odenton because they played the Frank Sinatra era songs, and Mom and I would whisper-sing all of the songs. Patrick would pretend he didn't know us, but that was hard to do sitting in a wheelchair at the same table with us. The last two years, Patrick missed four dinners because he was sick in the hospital, and I refused to leave him. He enlisted his brother, Marty, on those four occasions to pick up his mother and bring her to see him. Then, of course, on the way home, they'd stop for dinner.

After Patrick's dad died, Patrick took care of his mom's affairs, one of which was the blue Nissan stick-shift truck that his dad used to drive. He enlisted Lance to drive the truck because you must drive a vehicle or it will stop running and need massive repairs, and Patrick no longer had the strength to drive a stick shift. I recall riding on Route 100 and noticed a guy driving a blue truck with his dog sitting next to him in the truck. I thought how happy they seemed, and yes, it was Lance with his chocolate lab, Brandy.

Published

Because I married before I finished my degree, when I had the time and/or money, I attended college. I was working for The Widgets Testing Agency, Inc. when I was published in the Amaranth, which is the Anne Arundel Community College Magazine for the Arts. There was a writing contest. I thought the subject had to have something to do with blood. I may have been wrong. The other two students in my writing class had other students read their winning entrees out loud. I was told to read my own. I believe the teacher was happy with my story, but he figured another student would probably be embarrassed. It's a short story, titled, *It Begins.*

> I'm so excited. I just turned nine years old last week, and my dad and I are on our way to Aunt Eleanor's. She gives me great presents. Mom's going with Billy to a play rehearsal, so she can't come. I've really kind of glad. I'm still mad at her because she yelled at my birthday party. She said I was too rough on my little brother. She's always yelling at me. "Do your homework! Clean your room!" and on and on. I like being with my dad better than anyone else. He never yells at me. I'm his favorite. Oh, he loves Billy, but not nearly as much as me.
>
> I knew it. Aunt Eleanor gave me a doll with six outfits. The cake and ice cream were so good. My dad's still telling jokes, and everybody's laughing. He told everyone that I'm his very best girl.

My tummy's beginning to hurt. Maybe I ate too much ice cream? My underpants are kind of sticky. I better go to the bathroom and see what's wrong.

Oh, no. There's blood in my pants. Not a lot, but it is blood. Why am I bleeding? What's wrong? This is scary.

I'll ask my dad. No. He doesn't know anything about "down there." He doesn't know any girl stuff. Thank goodness it's almost time to go home. Mom will be home. I'll put some toilet paper in my pants and hope no one notices. I wish Mom were here. I want my mother.

Our Home

Throughout our marriage, Patrick used to say that the home was the purview of the wife. He was always okay with whatever décor was in our home. While he took care of the maintenance of our home and cars, he did not have anything to do with physically or mentally changing the look of our home, and that was good because I liked to do that. There is always an exception to the rule.

When the children were in their teens, I decided to install a pass-thru between the kitchen and the dining room because after five years, Patrick was still "going to do it." I started to cut the hole, and Patrick said to me that men cut holes in walls, not women, and he took the saw and finished the hole. Then we argued loudly for hours as he finished the hole. After a few weeks, I installed the shutters, the sill, and the trim. That was the only time I remember having a full-blown argument, and it was in front of the children. What's kind of funny about it was that we weren't really angry. Maybe we did it just for the experience of it? In an odd way, it was kind of fun. Our children didn't seem to be bothered, but it couldn't have been good for them.

College

A few years later, I attended the newly opened University of Maryland, Baltimore County Campus, who accepted all of my credits from Anne Arundel Community College, Towson State and Frostburg State. I finally graduated from the University of Maryland University College in 2003. Margot had brought her camera and was down to her last picture. Patrick, Margot, and Lance realized that Ray Lewis of the Baltimore Ravens was graduating on the same stage as I was. Ray Lewis said he had promised his mom he would finish his degree, and he did. Patrick and Lance wanted Margot to take a picture of Ray Lewis, but she used her last picture to take a picture of me graduating. Patrick and Lance were unhappy with her for days, but I was pleased. I was pretty sure Mr. Lewis didn't care one way or the other.

When I was working in D.C., I worked in a very nice office as a secretary. The Widgets, Inc. had an executive secretary's program. You had to take classes at your local community college and internal classes at work. Any college credits you already had could be counted in the college classes. It took me three years, but I earned the executive secretary title. I only had it for about one year when the executive secretary title was thrown out as every secretary became executive assistants. All that work for nothing, except there was an in-house secretarial class that helped me with just plain living. In the class, you had to write what you wanted put on your tombstone. The crux of the class was that no one wrote executive secretary, and we shouldn't have spent time worrying about the classes. Anyway, my tombstone inscription was, "She loved and was loved." Sometimes, when things go wrong, I think about that inscription and I feel better. I remember that even though we have to stay tough and keep going, we are loved.

Dad Passed On

Dad and Henrietta had moved back to Carroll County, Maryland, from Florida to her farm three years before my dad died in the nursing home. For the first year at the house, we would visit at least once every week, and the children would play their instruments for Dad and Henrietta—Margot, the flute, and Lance, the trumpet. They played very well by then, and I thought this was their musical gift to them for their listening to our children when they were first learning to play.

For the two years Dad was in the nursing home, Patrick, Margot, Lance, and I drove one and one-half hours each way to see him every Sunday, except one. The last time we came, we knew he was dying. He looked like a little animal in the bed. He was sort of scrambled looking with his arm stretched out and yet his fingers were clenched and his white hair was everywhere which meant the back and sides, because he was bald since he was twenty years old. I was afraid to hug him. I wanted to, but I just couldn't. I stood next to the wall, silently praying that God would take him home. I felt like a heel, but much to my happiness, Patrick hugged him, big time, with his arms wrapped around Dad's whole body. I have always been grateful to Patrick for Dad's big hug. When we returned home, we received a phone call that Dad had died. I never realized how much a funeral viewing could mean to a person because when I saw my dad in the coffin, the little animal was gone; he looked like himself. No, I did not kiss him goodbye.

Egg Babies

When Margot was in high school, she had to attend a parenting class. She was sixteen years old, five foot two inches tall, with a slim build, and had bottled blond hair which she usually wore parted on the side. She had beautiful shiny white teeth with the tiniest space between the two front middle ones, and shimmering brown eyes. The teacher in the health class gave each child an uncooked egg that they had to babysit—oops, eggsit—for one whole month. Monday, when she brought home her egg, she laid him in an egg carton bed that she had already cut in half and painted green. She covered him with yellow Easter basket grass for his blanket. She drew for him huge brown eyes, a ski-sloped nose, blond hair, and some shiny white teeth with a tiny space in the middle. She had wanted it to be a girl, but couldn't think of any really nifty egg-girl names, so she named him Eggbert—an exceptionally cool name for an egg baby.

That afternoon she asked me, her mother, to watch Eggbert while she played soccer. I agreed to egg-sit. After the game, she asked me, "Mom, where's Eggbert?"

"I'll get it." During the game, I'd left Eggbert on the dashboard of my friend's car.

"Mother, what kind of a grandmother are you going to be?"

Thursday, with great trepidation, she asked, "Mom, will you watch Eggbert for me? I have soccer practice till 6:30."

I said, "Okay, I'll do it."

Margot said, "Mom, you'll watch him all the time, won't you?" I assured her that I would be real careful with it. Margot and I both wore an ear-to-ear grin when she finally returned her well-cared-for Eggbert to her teacher.

Three years later, Lance had to egg-sit. Lance had hair so white you could hardly see it. He had just reached his tallest height of six feet. He was thin and had an all-day smile. Between his short hair, fair skin, hazel eyes, and white teeth, sometimes you couldn't see him in the sun. When he received his egg, he got a small box, lined it with plastic bubble wrap, and placed the egg baby in it. He did not name his egg. When Margot asked him about his egg, he said, "I am not going to name it. I am not going to copy you by painting a face on it. Unless I'm carrying it in my knapsack during school or at football practice, I will keep it on the top shelf of my closet. Most egg babies *sleep* a lot, Margot."

Margot asked him, "Lance, what kind of father are you going to be?"

"A happy and rested one!"

I never had to egg-sit for Lance, but Lance and I still wore ear-to-ear grins when at the end of the month, Lance gave back the original egg baby to his teacher.

Speaking of eggs reminds me that every Easter, our children and some of their friends would dye Easter eggs in our kitchen for my Sunday school class Easter egg hunt. I boiled the eggs and they dyed them. One year, Tim, one of their friends, decided to write with the crayon words like "Happy Easter," "666," and "The devil's looking at you," etc. I couldn't believe he did that, but I had Easter egg wraps, so I put the wraps around the eggs and dunked them in boiling water so the wraps would adhere to the eggs. Who knew that when the children found the eggs at the egg hunt, that the wraps would come off? What a Sunday that was. We played egg-pick. One child would try to break the other child's egg by banging the small end of an egg onto the large end of another egg. The child's egg that broke, lost and the winner got to play with another child. By the end of the game, all of the eggs were broken, and there were none for the children to take home. I was successful in that no one knew what happened. I wonder if the church folks would have kicked me out of church if they'd seen those eggs? Every year after that, I boiled twice as many eggs and only allowed our children and their friends to write offensive stuff on one-half of the eggs. I also checked every egg taken for the hunt.

Teenage Drivers

Margot was sixteen years old when she became old enough to drive. Margot took her driver's license test on her birthday and passed. I recall the motor vehicle tester telling me that she hated when parents brought their children in on their birthday because lots of times, they failed. I'm glad Margot passed. We bought her a used Chevy Mazda. It was yellow and built like a little tank. That car saved her life. She was sitting at a stop sign when a county truck hit something and rolled over her in the car. There was a man sitting in a truck behind her, and he said he thought she had died. We didn't get much for the car from the insurance company. A friend suggested that we lie and say Margot had nightmares or something like that so we'd get more money, but we didn't do that. We figured she was all right with no problems, and we weren't going to mess with that. We bought her a used red Fiero sports car. It was always in the shop, but she liked it. Her boyfriend at the time had an extra car that she used regularly so she could deal with the shop time.

Margot drove Lance to school after she got her license. She also drove her best friend every morning to school with Lance. Margot and Lisa enjoyed taking him with them. They talked about girl stuff and about who was doing what to whom. Lance wanted the ride, but he usually came home red-faced, leaping out of the car and running in our house.

Three years later, when Lance came of driving age, we made him wait a few months, thinking about what the motor vehicle tester had said. He passed his first time too. We bought him a used Chevy Mazda "tank." It looked like Margot's car, except that his was black and white. He traded it right away for a V-8 used Chevy Mazda, also black and white. Judy, my friend, told her husband that Lance needed some help in fixing up his car. Bob, who was ancient by now, at least in his late eighty's, helped Lance get that piece of junk car spiffed up and on the road. It was so powerful that when Lance drove it to Frostburg with some of his friends, he got a huge speeding ticket. Patrick then had to hire a lawyer so Lance wouldn't lose his license. It cost us a hefty amount of money, so Patrick was not happy. But Lance and his friends were okay, so we were okay.

While Bob was helping Lance with his car, he told me about a sports car he thought we might use for parts for Margot's Fiero. It was a '70s red midget MG convertible sports car. It had a hole in the gas tank, but it ran. We bought it and instead of using it for parts, used it for fun. The children drove it too. I recall Margot and I on our way home from shopping in the Glen Burnie Mall, picking up Lance on the Glen Burnie ramp. He was sitting there, hoping someone would come by because the car ran out of gas. Patrick always said he never cared about having a sports car, but he had the car fixed and never complained to me about the expense when he and Lance broke down in that car on their way to work when they both worked at The Widgets Testing Agency, Inc. in Washington D.C. He liked riding in that car. It was a little car but made for a tall person. The gas petal was way in the front of the car, but I loved driving it too. The biggest problem was that you couldn't fill up the gas tank all the way because of the hole, so sometimes you ran out of gas. Oh, well.

Bucket List

Things you wish for but don't believe you'll ever get to do is a bucket list. One of my "bucket list" things to do was to visit Europe. When Margot finished high school, I took her to London for a three-day trip. I tried to get Patrick to go, but he said it was too much money, and he wasn't going. I wanted him to go so we could visit the Isle of Wight, which is where his family originated. He missed a good time. Margot and I did not visit the Isle of Wight, but we saw all of the London sights.

On advice from some of my coworkers, we tried to sleep on the plane so that we would be awake and ready to go when we reached London. We left our bags in a closet at the hotel because we were too early to check-in. Then we got a ride on a double-decker bus. It was hard keeping our eyes open, but we did. By eight in the evening, their time, we were ready for bed. The hotel elevator was broken, so we climbed the stairs. It was hot weather, so we opened a window in our room. There was no air-conditioning. There were two beds, one shorter than the other, and the bathroom was missing the top of one of the walls. It was a dump, but we only slept there. We unsuccessfully tried to watch television because after all, they speak English, but not American English, and we were tired.

The next day, we saw the changing of the guards at Buckingham Palace, and we rode on the "tube," or as we know it, the subway, to get there. We saw the Tower of London, Big Ben, and the Theatre District, and enjoyed eating scones with clotted cream.

On the plane ride home, they played the movie, *Independence Day*. Every time it comes on television, I watch it and smile because I remember our London trip.

More School

Even though I worked in Washington, D.C., I would take vacation time and come home early to surprise my children, you know, to keep tabs on them. Anyway, one day, I came home to find Lance and Samantha on our sofa, watching TV, when they both should have been at school. I asked them why they were there. Samantha said that her mother knew that she'd dropped out of school. I asked Lance if this was their new habit—staying home and goofing off. "Oh no," said he. "I'm still going to school." Un huh. You know when they're lying but you can't prove it until they flunk out.

Once he flunked out of college because he didn't attend, and because he was too busy spending time with Samantha on our sofa, Lance got a job with The Widgets Testing Agency, Inc. As his dad and I explained to him, "In this house, you're either a worker or a student." Even as a student, he and Margot had to hold down part-time jobs because they needed spending money; and when they got their driver's licenses and cars, they needed to buy gas for their cars.

In high school, Margot worked at Wendy's. She hated the grease and said that her complexion was becoming a total zit—you know, a huge pimple. I explained to her that as a teenager, a job was not a career. It was just to make money. So Margot got another job at K-Mart and then at a check-printing company, and when she was tired of that job, she got two different jobs at other check-printing companies.

Lance's first job in high school was as a paperboy for the *Gazette*. The *Gazette* supervisor delivered the papers each morning in his car before dawn, and Lance put the papers on his bike and delivered them to the neighborhood in the back of ours. Patrick helped Lance put plastic bags on the newspapers in inclement weather and drove

him around his route when it rained. I took him around to the cul-
de-sacs in his newspaper route neighborhood when he collected the
money. He never had any trouble, but I worried that someone might
try to take his newspaper money.

Lance's second job was as a fish guts sweeper at the local seafood
restaurant. He had turned sixteen years old, and we gave him a car.
We paid for the insurance, but he had to maintain the car and to
put gas in it. So he needed a job. He worked weekends and one or
two days during the week. He used to smell of seafood, grime, and
soap when he came home. In between sweepings, he got to wash the
dishes. He was tired when he got home. He too worked for K-Mart
for a year or so, and he still played football in high school and had
lots of friends.

Weddings

When Lance turned eighteen years old, he moved out of our house into an apartment with his girlfriend and her girlfriend. After a while, he moved back with us, but this time, we made an apartment for him in the basement because we believed he needed his own space. Just a few months later, he moved out again, then back again. Then at twenty-one years old, he married Samantha, moved out, and hasn't lived with us since.

They were married at our church. Samantha looked beautiful in her handmade dress, walking down the aisle. One of Samantha's friends was a seamstress and gave her the beautiful dress as a wedding gift. Lance had a fever blister, which he successfully covered up. Even so, he looked quite handsome in his tuxedo. Samantha's mom worked at the college and was able to book St. John's College as the reception venue. It was a huge room, beautifully decorated. There was tons of delicious food and a professional DJ. Everyone had a lot of fun dancing, talking, and eating.

About six months later, Margot moved out into an apartment. She was living with Luke. She'd met him while bar tending, which was where she worked when attending college. He had a dry wall business—LukesCo—and he was an artist when it came to dry walling. Actually, he was really good with most anything that needed to be done around the house.

Luke had a daughter named Cassidy. I've only seen her picture because she died in an automobile accident while exiting the school bus from the elementary school. She was Luke's only child. The death of a child usually pulls a couple together or pushes them apart. As my dad would say, "There's nothing worse than losing a child." My friend, Flo, liked to embroider clothing. She embroidered a sweatshirt for me with my three granddaughters' names and angel wings on the front. She had put what she thought was a mistake—angel wings—on the back of the shirt. I just think that was for Cassidy.

Tweety

A few months later, Margot called to say that someone had brought a litter of kittens to the bar where she worked and asked if anyone wanted them. There was one left. He had scruffy hair, was all dark gray, except for the white hair that looked like a bow tie on his neck under his chin. The problem was that he, nor his siblings, was old enough to be taken from their mother.

"Mom, do you want him?"

"Yes."

Margot named him Tweety. When I took him to the vet for his initial check-up, I added Bird. The vet said that was cruel. I thought it was funny, but I never called him Tweety Bird. That was just for the vet records. I didn't want Tweety to have a complex. He had to be bottle-fed, and I must admit, I did like holding him as I fed him his bottle. The only problem with bottle-fed kittens is that they usually become crabby cats.

Mom Mom and I Babysitting

After they married, Lance went back to school, part time, and got his degree while still working at The Widgets Testing Agency, Inc. After he did that, he decided to "go for" his master's degree. Samantha's grandmother, Mom Mom, and I came on Saturdays to watch the two girls because Samantha worked on Saturdays as a hair stylist. Her specialty was color, and because of her, her mom, Adriana, and I always had the best-looking frosted blond hair around.

Samantha wanted to return to being a hair stylist and worked part time. The evening part time was on Wednesdays, and I was tickled to be able to babysit for her because at my job, I was able to leave two hours early on Wednesday's and make up that time by staying two hours late on Fridays.

As soon as Lance was finished with his first class, he quit, so he no longer needed Saturday babysitters. He wanted to be with their girls, and I thought that was a good thing. I can still remember him pulling Chloe and Jocelyn's wagon with the two of them sitting inside, waving the Miss America wave at the neighbors, their forearms bent upward at their sides with only that hand twisting from side to side. Like Patrick, Lance spent lots of time caring for his children, but unlike his dad, Lance changed many diapers.

More College

Just this year, Lance got his master's degree. Woohoo. It was a lot of work and time. He waited to go back to school when all three of his daughters were teenagers because teenagers have a greater propensity for sharing their parenting time. Of course, you have to check on them periodically. I believe the teenage years are a weaning time. That little toddler you wouldn't trade for all of the gold in the world is easier to send off to college or a trade school, and then to give away to some guy for a wife.

Margot also had her missteps with college. Unlike her brother who took eight years to graduate, she took ten years. After her fourth year, we were expecting her to graduate, but she hadn't attended very well her fourth year because she was going to change her major for the third time. So she flunked out. Well, UMBC told her that after taking two classes at the community college, they'd let her back in to finish her degree. Margot took the classes, moved to Virginia with Luke, got a job in a library, and after a few years, finished her degree. Then she got a job working in advertising, and she and Luke married.

They had the wedding in Virginia, at a house on a lake. Patrick, wearing a tuxedo, walked Margot down the steps from the house onto the lawn to the lake. She looked beautiful in her A-line bridal gown. She'd bought her veil from a thrift store because it was beautiful, and it was something old. Her dress was new, the handkerchief was borrowed, and her garter was blue.

Luke's uncle was a preacher, and he married them. After Margot and Luke exchanged their vows, they held the reception on the porch of the house on the lake. They had a musical combo play on the lawn. Everyone laughed, danced, and ate. The weather was wonderfully warm and the venue, beautiful.

Christmas Tree

That Christmas, we were truly empty nesters for the first time. I put up a two-foot tree on the knee wall between the kitchen and the family room. It was decorated and had lights. Margot almost had a cow when she saw it. "Mom," she said, "you always said that Grandma and Granddad should put up a tree even though the children are grown, and you have an almost non-tree. Shame on you."

She was right. Patrick was still walking, so there was no reason for me to cheat on putting up a tree. Even today, I still put up a tree—artificial—but at least five or six feet tall. This year, it was white with colored lights and of course, lots of decorations. I leave the tree up until right before Easter. I turn it on every night, and if the weather's not sunny, in the day too. The good memories and the prospect of today's memories make me feel good.

Moving Again

After Lance and Samantha were married about five years, Samantha was pregnant again, and she and Lance decided that they needed a bigger house. They had purchased a three-bedroom rancher not far from her mom and us. Patrick was having a terrible time using the stairs in our split-level home, so we decided to purchase each other's homes. So our youngest granddaughter, Libby's, first home was our old home.

Our new home was white with a fairly large yard, large enough to let dogs and cats run around the yard, chasing the foolishly brave rabbits that happened to roam inside the fence. There were a couple of flower gardens that I learned how to not weed. If you mulch well enough, you could sit in the middle of the flowers, reading and drinking lemonade instead.

When you enter our new home, you must first pass the Beagle mailbox. It may be wood and tin, but it does look like a beagle. Once you pass the mailbox, you'll go up one step to the Goose. I loved to dress up the cement goose. Once inside, in the winter, we could have hot chocolate in front of the gas fireplace. In the summer, we could sip tea and eat cookies on the screened porch or just swing on the porch swing.

When you buy a new-to-you home, you want to make it your own; and when you buy a new-to-you home from your family, you really want to make it your own. Lance and Samantha installed a new kitchen, put in an on-suite bathroom, a new patio, a pool, and on and on. Patrick and I installed a new sunroom. That was a lot of fun. We didn't actually do any work. Patio Enclosures did that. We stood on the new cement floor, checked the framing, and reveled at how good everything looked. I particularly liked the roof skylight. Patrick liked that he didn't have to install anything. We had to put on a rubber roof after it was built because the rain was so loud on the roof that you couldn't hear the television. Once that was done, it became our favorite room, primarily because it was large and full of light; and even when Patrick had to use the power chair, he fit easily in there.

Still Vacationing

Around 2004, Margot, Luke, Lance, Samantha, Chloe, Jocelyn, Libby, Patrick, and I started vacationing together. Each family paid their own way. We did this for two years. First, we went on a cruise to Canada. The stewards made our beds and left towels on top folded into animal shapes. We swam in the pool on the deck of the ship where some little girl came up to me and sneezed on me, and then the water got warm. Seems she was sick. I wish her mom had kept her in bed. We saw the shows and visited the auctions onboard. Luke took Patrick golfing so that Margot and I could go ashore and see the hilliest area I have ever seen. We had a good time, but on a cruise, you don't get to see as much of the country like you do on a walking bus tour. But if you're tired and need a rest, cruising is the way to go.

The next year we went to Disney World. We flew to Florida and stayed at Disney in the Animal Kingdom. We each had our own rooms. From Lance and Samantha's room, you could see live giraffes, which was pretty exciting. They had an outdoor pool, which I swam in, but kept an eye out for little children and made sure they didn't get too close. We rode on a small train from the hotel into the amusement park. We got to visit with the princesses and rode great rides. We had breakfast with Tigger. We also visited the water park and saw Shamu the wale, but Libby thought his name was Shampoo, so forever more we called Shamu, Shampoo. Patrick was in his power chair, but he rode slowly, so we put Chloe on his lap, and she drove quickly enough to keep up with the rest of us. Chloe liked driving, and Patrick liked having a chauffeur. All good.

Every summer, for three days and two nights, Patrick and I would take the granddaughters on vacation to Williamsburg, or Ocean City, or somewhere close. We always had a good time, except

129

for one year when we booked a ritzy hotel room at Ocean City. Everyone was sick, except me. The only fun thing we did was to swim in the indoor pool. That didn't stop us from going on vacation together the next year and having fun.

Anna and Tobias

Vacations are wonderful, but if you work for a good company and with good people, working can be wonderful too. My boss's wife used to call every workday to speak with Tobias. I, as the secretary, got to speak with her first and I very much enjoyed doing so. We always discussed our families—husbands and children. We agreed that we had, probably, the two finest husbands ever because they cared for their families first. I guess you could say that they were family men.

One time, we had a series of conversations about Anna and Tobias purchasing a new car. Well, he got the one he wanted, and I teased Anna because she didn't get the RAV4 she wanted. After a few months, she did get the RAV4; and we laughed that, in the end, we always got our way, which was pretty much true.

The Widgets Testing Agency, Inc. offered a program which paid in time and money for the completion of a college degree. You had to possess at least a B average and be a senior. I had that, so I applied. Here's the rub. I was fifty-five years old and therefore, my company would not get the many years of bang for their buck, so to speak. Your office had to support your application. Tobias had retired, so I was a little concerned that I really didn't have anyone to fight for my position. I shouldn't have worried because the human resources person in the main office spoke up for me. She said that all soon-to-be and new mothers received a nine-month leave of absence with pay and that surely they could accommodate me for nine months of school. I didn't know about that until I graduated. I have always been grateful to Charlotte.

While I was away at school, Anna died. She had had cancer and, because he had retired, Tobias had the privilege of caring for her. I didn't receive the usual memo saying Anna had died; instead, I received an email with a copy of the newspaper notice. The advertisement next to Anna's notice was for a RAV4. So I knew she was happy and that she was in God's hands. Miracles happen every day. We just have to be open to seeing them.

Teaching Sunday School

I taught Sunday school for thirty-five years, mostly at Armiger United Methodist. After about twenty years, a lady wanted to teach the third grade, which I had been teaching. So I decided that it was unfair of me to keep having the fun, and I quit at the end of the year. But as one of our members, Harold said to me when I volunteered to teach another Sunday school class at the beginning of the next year, "When the fire bell rings, the horses line up." Not very flattering, but true. That's how I wound up teaching the teenagers. They actually were a lot of fun. In addition to the weekly lessons, we tried to imagine how people lived during Jesus's time. We took walks around the fellowship hall, pretending to attend weddings, and other events. Every year, before Easter, I would close the fellowship hall doors and throw over a huge table, just like Jesus did in the temple. That made a lot of noise and scared a few people. A couple of years, we built arks, *much* smaller than, but proportionate, to the original.

One year, there were no girls in the class. What do you talk about with twelve boys? I bought the Hal Lindsey book, *The Late Great Planet Earth*. With the help of that book and the Bible book of Daniel, we read the book of Revelation, which is very scary, but the boys loved reading it. As usual, the teacher learned a lot, but I still don't understand it all.

Sunday's Children

There came a time after the children moved out that Patrick and I were "empty nesters." That was okay except that going to church was a lot less fun. I was still teaching Sunday school and working the picnics and other kid stuff, but it just wasn't as much fun without my own children. I had a wonderful friend, Jackie, whom I had known since she was little. She had three children, Nick, Olivia, and Lacey, in that order. I always tried to be careful of their grandparents' feelings and tried not to impose too much on their family gatherings, but Jackie and Ron let me sort of adopt their children on Sundays. I loved them all. I love them still. After church, we'd go to lunch, usually at a fast food place. The girls and I would do girl stuff after church, like draw, have tea parties, style hair, etc.

Nick, who was thirteen years old with black hair, thin, and very smart was close with Patrick. Patrick loved to talk sports so of course, they would discuss sports. We found out that Nick liked the new-at-that-time computer stuff. I bought a used computer, complete with floppy disks. Neither Patrick nor I could work the thing, but Nick could, and he would go to Patrick's den (used to be Lance's room) and play games on the computer.

Olivia was twelve years old and had a mothering personality. She was thin, had black hair, and was always running after a wayward child, or helping one of the Sunday school teachers.

She took great care of Lacey, her sister, who just turned nine years old. Lacey had auburn hair and freckles on top of her cheeks. She was thin, maybe a little skinny with a great smile.

Many times, we would all go downtown to the train museum, or ride the train from Baltimore to Frostburg, to the aquarium, to the movies, etc. Fun stuff.

Granddaughters

Two years after we started taking Jackie and Ron's children to church, Samantha became pregnant. Woohoo. She had a little girl whom she and Lance named Chloe. She was a preemie, and she was beautiful. She came home after about a week. Samantha's mom and Mom Mom were a great help to her. I was glad because while I like babies, I like them better when they're about a year old.

Jackie asked me if we were still going to take her children to church. Of course, the answer was yes, unless she objected, and I was happy that she didn't. After Chloe was a year old, we started taking her with all of us on Sundays. Olivia had always put Lacey's seatbelt on, and now she did the same with Chloe. She helped to make my Sundays joyously easy.

Nick was now around sixteen years old, and he decided to stop going to Sunday school. For a while, he would walk to church and meet us there. I didn't know if he felt outnumbered with the girls, or if he just developed new interests.

The next year, Samantha gave birth to another beautiful granddaughter, Jocelyn, who weighed nine pounds, six ounces. Chloe had dark brown hair while Jocelyn had red hair. After she was one year old, Jocelyn came with us. Olivia, always intuitive and motherly, took great care of her and the other two.

I was still teaching Sunday school, and Jocelyn would cry when I would go to the fellowship hall, so I tried teaching while holding her on my hip. It wasn't working very well, but I didn't want her to cry. Patrick came to my rescue. Every Sunday, he took Jocelyn to the kitchen, which was just behind the fellowship hall. They would have cookies and milk, and would go outside, sit, and watch the birds fly and the flowers grow. It only took a month or so for Jocelyn to join her Sunday school class, thanks to Pop Pop Patrick.

Three years later, another beautiful granddaughter, Libby, was born.

She had blond hair and weighed around six pounds. When she was a year old, she came with us, and Olivia mothered her too.

Brethren United Methodist

The next year, I asked Lance and Samantha, and Ron and Jackie if they would be all right with our attending another church. I had been in charge of the nurture committee which over saw the youth activities, which included the Sunday school run by my good friend Clair. I won't go into it, but our church was having internal conflicts, and Clair resigned from the Sunday school during the nurture committee meeting. I resigned the next day. I still stayed on as a Sunday school teacher, but in the fall, it was apparent that the new regime did not want anyone from the old Sunday school attending, let alone teaching. So I decided to find a new church home, only Patrick was not leaving. I left him there, took the girls, and went to Brethren United Methodist.

We'd only been there about two weeks when I realized that they did not have a children's choir. We had one at our old church, and I was feeling guilty because they would miss out being in the children's choir. I asked the preacher if he would mind if I started a children's choir there. He told me to wait just a minute. He went into his office and returned with a key to the church. He took me over to the church, showed me the secret to unlocking the door, and thanked me for volunteering.

Brethren United Methodist had two churches in one. There was a hearing church and a deaf church. I didn't know much about signing. I had given Lacey a sign language book for Christmas, but that was all I knew about speaking with the deaf. I shouldn't have worried because some of the deaf ladies ran a free sign-language workshop one night a week in one of the Sunday school rooms. They had some hearing friends who attended as well, Ms. Gail being one of the more notable ones, but there were others too.

We needed to learn to sign so that the children's choir could sign the songs at the deaf service as well as sing at the hearing service once a month. We tried having the choir sign and sing at the same time. We learned that they could either sign or sing, but not together. So they signed for the deaf church and sang for the hearing church. Both the hearing and the deaf church welcomed the children's choir. They were so receptive that it was an excellent experience for the children and for me too.

When the children's choir wasn't singing, we attended church. Olivia did her best to entertain the younger girls while sitting in the pew. I believed that they were pretty quiet, but not so because after a few weeks, the church opened up childcare in one of the Sunday school rooms during the service. Ms. Greeg was the lady in charge of the childcare. She had to be at least ninety years old. There was no way she could take care of little children; but Olivia, whom half of the church thought was Libby's mother because she usually had her on her hip or was running after her, could take care of everyone. What a wonderful thing for the church to do. The only children in the day care were mine. I didn't know who arranged it, but the girls loved going there, and Ms. Greeg loved being with them. When I would go to pick them up, she would tell me about all of their antics and show me pictures and other stuff the girls, with Olivia and Lacey's help, would make for her and to take home. It was a win-win for everyone.

Transportation Issues

We had purchased a green/blue Honda for our principal car to drive. Patrick and I took Olivia, Lacey, and Chloe everywhere in this Honda; but after Jocelyn was born, there wasn't enough room. Olivia had to put Lacey and Chloe in the same seatbelt. One evening while at home, I heard a big crash outside of our house. The girlfriend of the boy across the street backed out of their driveway and hit the driver's side front panel of our parked car. She came to get me, crying. The panel didn't look horrible, so I told her it was okay, and no one would notice the dent. But I noticed the dent all the time, so when we needed more room, I was happy to replace the Honda with a red Chevy Venture van.

The van was roomy, and when Libby was born, there was more than enough space to accommodate her. Olivia had no problem belting her in. We only kept that van for three years because it had 120,000 miles on it, because I worked one and one-half hours both ways from home. In retrospect, we should have kept it until it died. After all, it still ran great.

We traded the Chevy van for a blue Toyota van. I drove it today. In the first month, we had to have it towed twice to the dealership. It just wouldn't turn on. At first, they thought it might be the battery, and then there was something else. I knew they would fix it on the second try because after three strikes, Toyota would have to replace the van. They got it to start, but even today, you still have to move the steering wheel that quarter inch or so, or it won't start. At first, I was peeved, but then I thought a thief wouldn't know that, so I was okay with having to strain to move the steering wheel. We had a handicapped seat installed. It moved outside the van and down so that Patrick could scoot from his power chair onto the seat, and then the seat would lift him up and into the van. Modern technology is a wonderful thing.

The Blizzard

Through the years, the girls became close and gave me many laughs. A few times, we had sleepovers. We had a blizzard one year and got snowed in at our house. We put Patrick in the den, where he stayed. He was happy because no one was allowed in the den. The girls all slept in their room (the guest room), like usual on the floor in their sleeping bags, but during the day, "Ms. Olivia and Ms. Lacey taught school." They had had a friend spend the night with them, so there were four "students." They walked back and forth between the "teachers room" (the sunroom) and took instruction from their "teachers." I made sure there were food and drinks. We were snowed in for three days, and they had more fun than the law allowed. Although, I will say that by the third day, the girls were getting home sick. Nick came over and shoveled out a path to the street on the third day so their parents could pick them up. After they went home, Patrick and I sat together in the sunroom and enjoyed the quiet. Nevertheless, we were happy to see them again the next Sunday.

As Olivia and Lacey each turned eighteen years old, they found other interests and stopped attending church with Patrick and I. Olivia started attending church with her aunt, and Lacey returned to Brethren United Methodist Church of the Deaf and of the Hearing.

Chloe, Jocelyn, and Libby moved from Pasadena to Glen Burnie when Libby was sixteen years old. Chloe started attending a new church, and Jocelyn started attending college. I still picked up Libby, but after church, because terrible to admit, getting Patrick ready for church was never a sure thing as far as time went.

Old Vice Came to Haunt

I started smoking when I was twelve years old with my best friend and next-door neighbor, Nancy. We smoked in her bedroom. I can't believe her mom couldn't tell we were smoking in there, but she never said anything. We used to keep the window open so the smoke would go outside, and of course, we hid the cigarettes. In those days, it seemed as if everyone smoked, but your parents—smokers themselves—didn't like it when you smoked. My mom never smoked, but Dad loved smoking his cigars.

I wish I had never smoked because when I quit at thirty-eight years old, I gained forty pounds and never really lost it. Poor Patrick. I wasn't thin to begin with, and now I was fat. I told him I was sorry, and he told me that he was happy to be with me and to stop worrying. He reminded me that beauty was in the eye of the beholder and that maybe love was clouding his vision, but he thought I was still beautiful. What I loved was that he held me close when he said that.

Rocky

We were still attending Brethren United Methodist when Rocky was born to Lance and Samantha's cat, and he needed a home because Rocky had worse bathroom habits than Milo. Any item of clothing left on the floor, he urinated on. Sometimes, he just did not use the litter box, and if he asked to go out and didn't get his way quickly enough, he would urinate by the door. So Rocky became an outdoor cat. The vet wasn't too happy and frankly neither were we, but we just couldn't keep him in the house. He got along with Tweety who became an outdoor cat as well because we couldn't figure out how to put Rocky out and keep Tweety in the house. We never again used Peanut's green-jeweled collar and dog line on Tweety. However, probably because Tweety had been a house cat, he never seemed to go far from home.

After Rocky came to live with us, Margot called to say that a friend of hers needed a home for his dog. She was a beagle. Un huh. Just like Milo was a beagle, sort of. She was well trained. You could sit on the porch with her, and she would not leave your side. Walking in the yard, she walked with you. She was every bit as gentle and loving as Molly. She was about three feet tall, and she was beautiful. She had the beagle tricolors (brown, black, and white), but she did not have the beagle howl. She knew that Molly ruled, and Sasha was okay with that. The only problem Sasha had was her first week with Tweety. He chased her up and down the hall every chance he had. But the second week, Sasha chased Tweety back and forth. They formed some kind of truce after that. They weren't best friends, but they got along.

Rocky lasted eight years before he got run over. We found him under the bush on the side of our house. We took him to the vet, and they tried to save him. But they couldn't get his temperature up, so they couldn't operate on him and he died.

Patrick's Truck

While we had the Chevy van, we purchased a red Nissan truck for Patrick. By now, he used the walker exclusively to get around, and it was easy for him to pitch the walker in the bed of the truck. It was an automatic, had a nice radio, and was new; so I felt that he was as safe as we could make him on the road. After three years or so, he couldn't walk at all. Therefore, he couldn't work the pedals, so he couldn't drive the truck anymore.

Lance offered to buy his dad's truck. He'd made up a payment plan and had run it by Patrick. Patrick asked me what I thought. He could easily have accepted the payment plan from Lance, but Patrick liked to think he was frugal with his money like his dad was with him, but he wasn't. So he'd go with what I thought, which was what he wanted to do all along.

I watched a lot of the *Judge Judy* shows, and she recommended that if someone wants to borrow money and you have it, give it to them and tell them that it's a one-time thing. If you lend the money, you will wind up the bad guy. So I suggested to Patrick that since the truck was paid for, we'd just give Lance the truck. Patrick couldn't drive it anymore, and I'd have to drive it on the road once a week to keep it in good shape, so it made sense. Patrick thought that was a good idea, and it worked really well.

Our granddaughters each drove the truck as their first vehicle, and Libby drives it still. I know that Patrick was happy that the truck didn't go to waste. I believe that every time they drove it, they intuitively thought of their Pop.

After we gave Patrick's Nissan truck to Lance, we purchased a used green/blue Dodge Ram handicapped van. It was a 2005 but only had 12,000 miles on it, and the entire time we had it, the van was in excellent condition. Patrick could no longer drive a vehicle. He was beginning to have difficulty with transferring from one place to another. We had purchased a swing-out seat for the Toyota, but he couldn't make the transfer anymore, so we got a van with a ramp. He no longer had to transfer, and better still, we put the passenger seat in the shed so he could roll up the ramp into the passenger's area and ride next to me. In the next three years, we put an additional 12,500 miles on the van. We still took the granddaughters to church, to lunch, and to the Orioles baseball games because there was a full seat in the back of the handicapped van.

Anniversary Vacation

For our fortieth anniversary, we went to Hawaii. Patrick's Uncle Earl was on a boat in Pearl Harbor when we were attacked. Patrick loved listening to his uncle tell what happened that day. I knew he would like to see the places that Uncle Earl described.

We had a really good time. While Patrick usually rode in the power chair, on vacation, he could still, with a little help, use his walker to transfer from the power chair to the seat in the boat we rode from the shore to the Pearl Harbor Memorial. Patrick joined the Pearl Harbor Memorial that day, and until he died received information and bought stuff from them. We went on several riding tours and saw pretty much all of the Oahu Island.

The only negative was that I hadn't done my homework well enough, and we didn't know about the cruise that went to all of the islands. In retrospect, that cruise may have been too much for him to handle. Instead, there was a boardwalk next to our hotel extending from the beach to maybe twenty feet over the water, so Patrick got to sit over the water and I gently splashed him with the water. We always had fun when we were together.

Molly's Gone

About three months after we returned home, Molly died. The vet said she had cancer and that we were lucky that she had not been and was not in pain before she just fell asleep and died. We were very distraught. Patrick called his minister, Douglas, who volunteered to pick up Molly's remains from the vet hospital and then brought her to our house where he dug a grave, spoke words over her, and then filled in the hole. I decided then that it was time for me to go back to our church with Patrick. So we all came back, and now we had two church homes—Armiger United Methodist and Brethren United Methodist Church of the Deaf and of the Hearing.

Greatest Compliment

Our children honor us by becoming good and upstanding adults.

After Margot graduated from Northeast High School, she attended University of Maryland, Baltimore County Campus (UMBC). She also coached girls soccer for the Buccaneers. She remembered that when she was a player, the coaches told them to run, but the coaches never ran with them, so she ran with her players. Throughout the years, she's volunteered for many causes. The one that worried me the most was when she taught the adults to read. She'd meet them at the library or a coffee shop, and they'd read together. She never had any problems, so I guess I should not have worried.

Lance volunteered to coach his girls' sporting games. Patrick loved the many times he was Lance's assistant coach. The girls played basketball, soccer, and softball when they were little. Even when Patrick had to use his cane to walk, he still assisted at the softball practices and games.

I always attended the games and occasionally the practices. One day, when Chloe and Jocelyn were seven and eight years old, I was watching one of their softball games and as usual, cheering for the children. A young guy, who looked to be in his late twenty's walked across the field, around a couple of baseball diamonds to see me. He asked if I was Lance's mom. "Yes." He had come by to say that he remembered that I always rooted for everyone, even those on the opposing team. And then he thanked me.

Greatest Punishment

When the children were little, one of the things I hated to do was to punish our children; but if you want to raise good people, sometimes you have to punish them.

We had punished Margot in middle school because we thought, wrongly, that she wasn't studying for her algebra class.

We punished Margot when our neighbor said she beat up Lance when she watched him between the time that Patrick got home and when I went to work. Margot was not allowed to leave the yard for one week. That worked really well. That and the fact that Lance grew bigger than she, so he could defend himself.

We punished Lance by making him stay home in his room when he had been invited to a party. I felt so bad I was crying in the living room. Lance heard me and yelled, "I can hear you having fun."

We sometimes even have to punish our grandchildren. Our oldest granddaughters were having a fight in our van on the way home from church. We had been invited to a party after church, but since they were fighting, I told the two older ones that they would have to stay home with Pop Pop while the youngest and I went to the party.

After we left, the oldest, Chloe, called her mom and said that her middle sister, Jocelyn, was bad and had started a fight. I wonder if Chloe thought she would not be in trouble? After the party, our youngest, Libby, and I returned home to find that her dad, Lance, had picked up her sisters. When I returned our youngest granddaughter to her home, I encountered both of her older sisters painting their shed. I thought that was a marvelous punishment.

Bucket List Revisited

When Jocelyn, our middle granddaughter, was in high school, her teacher sponsored a twelve-day trip to Italy, Austria, Germany, France, and Switzerland. They were allowed to invite whomever they wished. I was thrilled to accept Jocelyn's invitation. We had a year to pay for the trip, and they had meetings telling us how to pack and what we'd see and when. There were extras too, like going through the Black Forrest and seeing the homes with pictures painted on them.

Patrick would have to stay thirteen days in the nursing home while we were on the trip. I thought about not going, but I knew they would take good care of him. One of my youth groupers, now an adult with a family of her own, worked in the nursing home office. I knew she would look after him, and on their own, the staff were great. It came to pass that Patrick had had a procedure in the hospital a few days before we left, and he had to recuperate in the nursing home for a few days. That lessened my guilt for leaving him there.

By now, I was lots older than when Margot and I went to London. I'd had both meniscus, one in each knee sewn, and I used a cane for long distances. These people on this class trip were some of the nicest people I have ever met. They didn't complain that I made the trip slower. What they did was to make sure that I was in the front of the group when we started walking so I'd be at the back of the group when we'd arrived at wherever we were going. A couple of the men, participants in the trip, called themselves "sweepers" and came at the end of our group to ensure we all were there. They could have complained and been mean; but everyone was kind, nice, and happy to be there.

I made a friend that I seldom see because she lives across the country, but we still keep in touch. Her name is Buddy, and we were roommates on the trip. She's an early riser, so she'd get up, take her shower, and call me. She'd go down to breakfast, and when I was ready, I'd go down for breakfast. We'd sit together almost every day on the bus. Her daughter was one of the teachers, so she'd have dinner with her and the other adults. I was there with my granddaughter, so I'd have dinner with her and the other children. We had a wonderful time on my second trip to Europe. I'm happy to say that many times in life, you get more than you hoped for.

Sasha and Tweety— Both Gone

Two years later, Sasha died. We're not sure why, but after eight years, it was hard to let her go. She was sixteen years old, but we'd only had her for eight. I slept on the floor with her for her last night. Around three in the morning, she walked to the other side of my bed; and a short time afterward, she scooted between me and the bottom of the bed where she breathed her last breath. I was glad she came back to lie by me and would have been heartbroken if she hadn't wanted to be near me when she died. Luke came by in the morning and buried her in our backyard. We really missed her and thought about getting another dog. Soon after Sasha died, we were dog sitting Lance's two dogs, Fergie and Thor, in our yard when Tweety attacked them. I put my hand between them and got bit by Tweety. I had to get a tetanus shot and to come to the realization that Tweety was not ready for another dog or cat.

About one year later, Tweety started to urinate in the house, at first near his litter box, but then everywhere. He was nineteen years old, and we realized that, like Peanut, he was at the end of his life. He got real skinny and lethargic, and we took him to the vet who agreed with us that it was time for him to be put down. Now we were pet-less, and Patrick was really sick. He could only move his right arm a little, and the index, middle finger, and thumb on his right hand. There was no way he could help with a dog, but as any pet lover knows, a dog brings a lot of love to your house. So Libby, Jocelyn, Chloe, and I started visiting the humane society pound. We'd keep Jocelyn in the loop by cell phone because she had gone back to college.

More Dogs

After a few months, Libby found Roxy, named by Chloe. She was a beautiful, tricolored pocket beagle. She was smaller than a regular-sized beagle, but still a handful on the leash. She had been trained because she knew what "sit," "lay," and "come" meant. She also had great bathroom habits. Woohoo! The veterinarian never said anything about her being a pocket beagle. She was a nice dog, not mean; but when she got to playing, she sometimes bit. I guess that her previous owners probably had children and couldn't take the chance of them being bit during play. Roxy loved Patrick. When he was seated in his power chair, she would climb on the wheel so he could reach her and pet her. I took care of her, but she only "had eyes" for Patrick.

About six months later, Patrick's ninety-four-year-old mom fell and had to go into a nursing home; so we inherited Precious, a toy white poodle who had lived with his mom. She was untrained and had terrible bathroom habits. We worked with her and she got better, but she never became good with her bathroom habits until we got a pet door.

Just a week or so before Patrick went into a coma, he and I went to visit his mom at the assisted living care facility. She had fallen at home and needed assisted care, if only for a while. She'd only been in there about a week. She had been yelling at me. No, there didn't seem to be a reason. I believe she was just unhappy to be in the nursing home even though it was a lovely place and the employees were super nice.

So when we left, I said to Patrick, "Couldn't you have said the weather was fine or something else like that to get me off the hook?"

His response to me was, "I was just glad she was yelling at you and not me."

He was seventy-three years old and still afraid of his mother. I didn't realize that, but that did give me some insight into some things that happened in the past. Actually, I yelled at him—even near the end—because when our children were little, he took our children over to his parents' house after his mother told him I couldn't come. Here's what's worse. I was under the impression that she told Brad the same, and that he didn't go over there without his wife. Come to find out, he went for a while, but then he stopped. Yes, I can be a real heel.

Toward the End

Before he died, Patrick had had several autoimmune diseases. His body was frozen, except for two fingers and his thumb on his right hand, and a small movement of his right arm. He could still chew and swallow, so he could still eat by himself if he had small, bite-sized sandwiches; but that was the extent of his movement. A few years before, a therapist asked if we would like a lift. We were glad to have it. Once you lose the ability to transfer from the bed to a chair, or from a chair to a chair, you're stuck in the bed if you don't have a lift. Sometimes, maybe two or three times a month, I'd get him trapped in the lift, and we'd have to have the firefighters come and lift him out to the bed or the chair, depending on whether we were leaving or coming home. We learned that it wasn't necessary to have both the ambulance and fire department come because he wasn't hurt, just stuck. The firefighters from all of the three firehouses that used to visit us—Lake Shore, Armiger, and Riviera Beach—were always nice to Patrick. I was always grateful for them. Also, we got a handicapped van with a power ramp so he could drive the power chair up the ramp. Between the lift, the firefighters, and the van, he still got out of the house to doctor's appointments and attended family affairs, Orioles games, and church.

The last year or so, Patrick would receive home visits from nurses. They would take care of him for whatever disease at that time was ravaging his body. He even had a tech that would come to clean him and give him a shave every week. Just before she came the last time, Patrick threw up just a little. She said she couldn't clean him, so I said that was okay. I would take care of cleaning him. She looked at him and said, "I believe he needs to go to the hospital." I thought she was crazy, but thank goodness I listened to Mary because on the way to the hospital, in the ambulance, Patrick slipped into a coma and never came out of it. When I left the hospital, around three in the morning, I saw the sign and only then realized that Patrick was in intensive care. I felt like an idiot because I kept telling him to wake up. Early the next morning, the hospital called Samantha, and she came and banged on my window. We got everyone together and went to the hospital, but he didn't die for a few more days.

They tried several things, but Patrick was only breathing five percent, and nothing else was working. The day he died, we prayed for him, and then the doctor came in and we gathered around Patrick. Lance held his left hand and stood next to the machine. I held his right hand. Samantha stood next to me. Margot was next to Samantha at the foot of the bed, and Luke stood next to Margot. The doctor "pulled the plug." No sooner had the doctor left the room, he came right back in because Patrick had passed that quickly. The death certificate said Multi-System Failure. That made sense to me. I believed that when the outside of the body was freezing up, so was the inside.

My husband, Patrick, died after forty-eight years of marriage. He had been sick with Sjogren's syndrome, transverse myelitis, polio, Reiter's disease, lupus, and rheumatoid arthritis. He had had an appendectomy, setting of a broken leg, removal of a joint of his big toe, and nerve endings cut in several of his toes, first when in his twenties. At birth, he weighed nine pounds. He was diagnosed with polio at the age of five, although he denied any history of paralysis or paresis. He received his bachelor's degree and a master's equivalency. He thought that he excelled in history and was weakest in math. He was a college-educated paralegal specialist with The Widgets Testing Agency Inc. Previously, he worked as a teacher in the elementary school system for twenty years and retired on disability as a result of left ankle destruction of cartilage secondary to the Reiter's disease. He was in the Air Force for six months and received an honorable discharge as a result of foot problems unrelated to the Reiter's. He had always been a worrier, and had a tendency to worry regarding the potential complications of his medical conditions.

He smoked for about three years in his early twenties. He consumed at least two pots of caffeinated coffee per day until he was in his fifties, cut back to one pot a day, and by age sixty, gave up drinking coffee.

Numbness began after he received a flu shot on October 24, 1998. He also started to have concentration and alertness problems. He said he didn't have as good a memory as before, but he did. On October 31, 1998, he had an onset of right-sided numbness that was initially felt to have been related to a stroke or transient ischemic attack (TIA).

The Funeral

Patrick died on May 17, 2015. Part of me was cheering because he'd made it to be with God and Jesus, and part of me was missing him sorely. We had a viewing at the Stalling Funeral Home on Thursday of the following week and a service for him the next day, Friday, at the church. It was as wonderful as it gets for a funeral. Because so many people came, they had to put extra pages in the viewing book on Thursday, and the church was full on Friday. The preacher spoke about Patrick keeping his Chevelle long after it should have been junked.

Then Lance spoke, and you could feel the love he felt for his dad. He teased about Patrick being frugal and told stories about Margot and he having to retrieve their dad when he broke down in the Chevette—not the Chevelle—downtown occasionally. And he told about Patrick dragging back in the old worn-out sofa from the sidewalk where we had put it for removal before Patrick got home from work. He told how his dad stayed after church almost every Sunday, counting the collection money with the counters and cleaning the church kitchen and other duties because "someone had to do it." Then Chloe spoke. She said she would try not to show up her dad. She spoke about Patrick being her "bestest buddy." Then she sang a song, "Heaven Must Have Needed a Hero" by Jo Dee Messina, with her beautiful voice and brought tears to almost everyone.

Jackie, then spoke about Patrick having her help him find a bumper in the newspaper ads and how he'd said he thought he could get it even cheaper than the advertised price. Then a lady he worked with at Widgets spoke about what a good worker and kind friend he had been. She spoke for quite a while, and we were happy to meet her. The Ladies Society prepared a huge luncheon for all of those in attendance. It was a wonderful wake. Everyone ate and talked about the old days before Patrick got really sick and reminisced about when we were young and the children were too.

Margot put a picture on Facebook of Luke, Patrick, and Lance sitting around her counter while talking together. She lovingly wrote, "My father, Patrick Wightisle, died yesterday morning. He was a good father, and a good person, and I miss him. He suffered terribly in the last few years of his life, but now he is free."

Pepper and Marty brought Patrick's mom from the nursing home, and she kept looking for Patrick. I believe she knew Patrick was gone, but she'd rather not think that way. No one wants to out-live their children, no matter how old they are.

When we were newly married, we watched a movie with Ernest Borgnine as a husband who died and who laid in the bed with his widowed wife to make her feel better. I made a pact with Patrick that whoever died first would *not* lay in the bed with the other living one. How creepy and scary that was to me.

Something had been nagging at me on Thursday and Friday. I kept thinking about how much I loved being hugged. I couldn't figure out what it was until Saturday because Saturday, it stopped. I realized I had been "hugged" for those two days. I felt so good. I believe it was Patrick's way of saying, "I'm okay. I love you. You took care of me the best you could, and that's okay."

I tried my best, but I know in my heart of hearts that I could have, should have, taken better care of him. I should have exercised his limbs more. I put my face next to his and put my head on his chest from outside of the bed, but that didn't work. We used to lay in our bed, my back to Patrick's chest, and talk at least a couple of times a week. So I tried lying in the hospital bed with him. I had a hard time getting out of the bed. We might have been stuck in the bed until someone came, so I only tried that once. Sometimes, I'd go to bed during a TV show, and he'd have to call me to turn off the TV. But he let me off the hook. Thanks, Cutie.

The Aftermath

Patrick's gone and I miss him. I think about him all the time. The other Sunday, Leann asked me if I'd help count money because two of the money counters went on vacation to Ocean City. I said, "okay." Well, I sorted the envelopes while the two regular money counters set-up the adding machines and other paraphernalia. I began to write the amount of money on the envelopes, and then I sought to balance the checks and cash with the marked envelopes. But I was five dollars short or over. I could not get it to balance. Jenna suggested that I put the money and/or checks on top of each envelope. I told her I thought that was smart, and she told me, "Your husband showed us how to do that." I didn't cry in front of them. I wanted to. Where was Patrick when you needed him? Gone to a better place, but I still miss him. I have a friend who said she cried a lot each day after her husband died. I don't do that very much. I think about him all the time, but I don't usually cry like I'm doing now, thinking how my husband taught these ladies an easy method for reconciling the envelopes. He must have done it using his usual easygoing teaching skills.

Patrick and I were married for forty-eight years before he died. I've seen many couples much older than Patrick and I, and married for many more years. I understood how they seemed to express their love for one another without saying so, or even physically demonstrating it. The way they looked at each other and just seemed to care for each other, waiting patiently or smiling with their eyes when they saw one another. It occurs to me that the saying, "Grow old together," makes sense. When you marry, the preacher says you're one. You don't physically become one, but you do grow to be one person in caring for and loving the other person. You in essence do become one, or a couple. When people invite you to a party, they don't invite Patrick or Penelope. They invite the Wightisle's. People view you differently. They think of you as Patrick's wife, or Penelope's husband. Instead of seeing how your mate looks physically, you see them as who they actually are. You care about your mate more than you care about yourself. Even when your spouse becomes disabled, you can still talk or just sit with and enjoy the company of each other. It's nice to have a person who's always in your corner. They may not always agree with your thinking, but they will back you when others come against you, no matter what. When Patrick and I used to come home after an activity, even though Patrick couldn't move, we would still sit in the van and talk about what we thought about everything, silly or important.

When your spouse dies, you are no longer a couple. You are only one person. You are single. You are lonely. That's coming from a woman who has a great support system. I have family and friends who are close to me. Through the years, our relationships have changed, as have our circumstances, but we're still together. I have to count the dogs who live with me and keep me going because I have to care for them. There's a lady I know from the fast food restaurant whose husband died right after Patrick. I said to her that I was grateful for all the support. She said to me, "What support?" I may be lonely, but I need to be more grateful for the loving support and the many blessings God has given to me.

A Test Case

In Jesus's day, when a man died, his brothers married his wife. A lady's husband died, and his seven brothers in succession, after their brothers died, married her. The priests asked Jesus which one would she be married to in heaven. Jesus said, "None of them because when you die, you are no longer married." This bothers most of us widows. We loved our husbands and want to be with them again. We know, though, in our heart of hearts that heaven is different from Earth. Jesus says heaven is wonderful and tries to describe it to us, but it's the same as a sighted person trying to describe the color blue to a totally blind person.

Throughout your entire married life, there is change. Children are born, you grow older, you physically move, etc.; so it makes sense that your relationship would not be the same. So I'm hopeful that I'll know Patrick again in some form or another when I see him there. In the movie *Ghost*, Patrick Swayze says you take the love with you. I'll bet that's true, but the ones left behind keep the love they have for the person who's gone. What's that old saying about the more you love, the more you can love?

More Aftermath

After about nine months, you move your wedding band to your right hand. Or like some of the other ladies, put yours and his bands on a chain around your neck because you're no longer married, but you don't want to be unmarried. Then one day, while doing the mail, you come to an envelope from a charity which included Mr. and Mrs. Patrick Wightisle return address stamps. And you cry. Here, you're thinking you're over the loss, and you realize you're not. You sit and cry. I would not wish Patrick to return. He was so sick, and I know now he's at home and feeling fine. But I'm feeling sorry for myself. I don't want to do that because I should be okay now, but I wonder if I'll ever stop missing him.

The Firsts

The first Mother's Day, I went to Margot and Luke's house for crabs, watermelon, and corn on the cob—three of my favorite dishes. Luke sat with us for a while after dinner, but then he fell asleep on the sofa, and Margot and I sat and talked about everything important to us. It was late when I got home, tired and happy.

The first Father's Day, I met Margot, Luke, Adriana, Chloe, Jocelyn, and Libby at Lance and Samantha's. We had a good time and ate a lot of crabs. Father's Day is hard for Luke. He lost his only daughter, Cassidy, when she was a school-aged child, but I'm glad to say he seemed to be okay sitting there with us.

The first Fourth of July, I met Margot, Luke, Lance, Samantha, Chloe, Jocelyn, and Libby at Billy and Julie's house who hosted us and their family. It was nice, but I was worried about Roxy, our pocket beagle who loved Patrick, and Precious, our toy poodle, being home alone. So I left before the fireworks. I shouldn't have worried. Roxy and Precious weren't bothered by the noise of the fireworks.

On Patrick's first birthday after he died, I signed up to substitute teach. The next day, Thursday, I showed up for work. The administrator assured me that I'd probably worked the day before and that she would check it out and I should stay that day too. Well, I stayed; and throughout the day, I realized that I'd not shown up on Wednesday. I left a note on her desk before I went home. It wasn't a good excuse, perhaps, but being confused because it was Patrick's birthday was the only excuse I had. I took a few months off from substituting after I messed up at the high school on Patrick's birthday. When I returned to substituting, the middle school principal, Mr. Johnson, put his arm around my waist and screamed, "*Wightisle's back!*" That really made me feel good.

The first Halloween, I got all dressed up as a witch and went to Oliver's (Addie and Kory's son) party. Addie and Kory were the only two people, except for Oliver's family, I knew; and they left not fifteen minutes after I arrived. I stayed about forty-five minutes, and then I left. I rode around the neighborhood a little bit because I just didn't want to go home. I thought about how nice it was that their whole family tried to look after me after Patrick died, and how I probably should have stayed at the party; but sometimes, I'd just rather be miserable by myself.

The first Thanksgiving, Margot, Luke, and I went to the Rusty Scupper which was always a nice place to dine. We had a really nice time, and it was easier without having to accommodate Patrick's power chair. Funny how I never minded the power chair and the commotion of getting it in the restaurant when it held Patrick, and how I missed the commotion.

The first Christmas, I picked up Patrick's mom from the assisted-living home and took her to Margot and Luke's for dinner. I'd done this for the past several years with Patrick in tow. I remember the first thing I said in the grace was that Patrick was not here with us this Christmas and Luke saying, "Don't cry." I didn't, but I wanted to. Patrick's mother said that Patrick wasn't there because someone had killed him at the store at which I worked. I didn't know where she got that from because I hadn't worked in a store for over ten years. Later, after dinner, Lonnie and Brad came by to see Patrick's mother. She hadn't seen Brad, Patrick's brother, in seven years. She didn't seem to know him. When I returned her to her assisted-living facility, she told the attendant that she'd seen her son, whom she'd not seen in years; so I told Lonnie, Brad's wife, so he'd feel better about the meeting. Lonnie said that he did feel better. After the assisted-living home, I went to Lance and Samantha's, and opened presents with them and Chloe, Jocelyn, and Libby. Then I went home and collapsed in my bed with the dogs.

The first New Year. We used to go to Billy and Julie's when the children were little. When Patrick became power-chair confined, we could no longer go. Billy called and suggested that I come over, but I didn't want to be on the road at night, alone. Lance called and suggested I come to his house, and Margot left me a voice mail inviting me to come play games at her home. I guess I was becoming a stick in the mud because I declined all the offers and stayed home, watching the New Year's ball plummet on television. A new year and no Patrick to share it with.

On Chloe's twenty-first birthday, Libby, Jocelyn, Chloe, Jake, and I went to dinner at the Mission Barbecue. I'd grilled Jake a little because he was dating Chloe. Afterward, Jake went home, so did Libby and Jocelyn. I went to Chloe's place of business, the Seaside Restaurant. Adriana, Margot, Luke, Lance, and Samantha met us there. Chloe and the rest of us had a couple of drinks. We had a few appetizers and dinner. Adriana paid the bill. All good. Thanks, Adriana.

Libby's sixteenth birthday. The next week, Lance and Samantha had a combined party for Libby who turned sixteen years old and the now adult, Chloe. They got lots of stuff and had lots of guests at their home. It was a fun time.

On my sixty-ninth birthday, Margot and I were supposed to go to a play, *Under the Skin*, but we had a huge snowfall. The theater postponed the play; so Margot, Luke, and I went to the Olive Grove for a delicious Italian lunch, and then we went home before the snow came down, hard. We were snowed in for three days. A couple of weeks later, we went to see the play and had dinner. We invited Luke to dine with us at Carmelo's, which had really good Italian food. Margot thought the play was good. I liked attending with Margot, but I thought the play was okay—funny in parts of it, but not funny enough.

The first Valentine's Day, I took Libby and her sort-of-boyfriend Reds to the mall. They went shopping while I looked for a spot to park. I wound up driving up to the top floor and down to the first floor of the parking garage just in time to pick up Libby and Reds. Seems Reds bought himself a gift, and Libby bought herself some socks. Afterward, I took them to Friendly's and treated them to dinner. Then I took Reds home and was on my way to taking Libby home when Reds called and said he'd left his gift to himself in the van. After I finished taking Libby home, I took Red's gift to him. He didn't thank me. I liked him before, but now a little less. I don't know if Valentine's Day was the reason, but I was glad that Libby got a new boyfriend, David.

The first St. Patrick's Day, Addie and Korey picked me up. They were supposed to bring their daughter, Janet, and her friend, Kenny; but Korey had a spat with Janet because she was late coming home from work. So just the three of us went to Johnny's restaurant for corned beef and cabbage. The food was good, but we left at five forty-five, and I was home by seven thirty in the evening. Korey called Janet to apologize, but we never recovered her return call. Kind of a bummer all around, but better than being home alone.

On my first trip, Addie, Korey, Janet, and I were supposed to go on a bus trip to see the Biltmore. This was on Addie's bucket list. Two days before we were supposed to leave, Addie got really ill and had to be hospitalized. We were not going to go on the trip, but after discussing our situation, we decided that because Addie would have to stay in the hospital for at least a few more days, and Melissa (her daughter-in-law) and Oliver (her son) would visit her there and take care of anything needing attention, we would go on the trip. Melissa and Oliver did an outstanding job. Everything went well with Addie's care. We had a good time on the trip. Korey and Janet made fun of the person who brought the checkers set for one of the gifts to be traded for the bus gift exchange. They had egg on their faces when they found out it was the gift I'd brought, but they still laughed, and I stuck out my tongue at them. Addie came home from the hospital just a few days after our return. Glad to say she's now well, but sad to say she never went to the Biltmore.

The first Easter, I picked up Addie while wearing sweat pants and a pullover sweater, and we attended the Easter sunrise service at six thirty in the morning. It was cloudy, so we didn't see the sunrise. But just being there singing and hearing the sermon started our day off with smiles and full stomachs because after the service, Kurtz's Beach provided us with scrambled eggs, sausages, breads, and pastries, plus juices, coffee, and tea. Thank you, Kurtz's Beach. After breakfast, I went home and got dressed. After church, I went to Margot and Luke's. Margot drove us to Renditions, a golf course having an Easter brunch. It was delicious, and I had a good time. We even got to take home some spicy marshmallow creatures, sort of like marshmallow ghosts at Halloween. I got home around four thirty in the afternoon. Since I'd been up since five in the morning, I was tired and almost went to bed, but I figured that was too early. So I napped in the recliner till nine o'clock and then called it a night.

Taxes. I put all of the correspondence for taxes in a big plastic bag as it came to our house in the mail. I forgot some of the charity stuff, but I got most of it. I was happy when the taxman was able to complete our taxes in one meeting. He was very nice and wrote Deceased in the signature box with Patrick's name. I had sold the handicapped van and had to write that word five or six times, and then Patrick's name. It was hard to do.

On Jocelyn's twentieth birthday, Lance and Samantha hosted a party for Jocelyn and her Aunt Barbara who turned thirty years old. Margot, Luke, and I came as well as Samantha's mom, Adriana. So, both her grandmothers were in attendance. They played corn hole, which used to be known as beanbag toss. There was plenty of fun and lots to eat. Jocelyn had to leave early the next morning for Salisbury. She was in a sorority and loved going to school. I believe the sorority had a lot to do with that. One of the fun things for me was that her sorority was somehow related to the fraternity that Patrick belonged to at Frostburg.

This was, I believe, the end of the firsts without Patrick.

It's All Over

I believe the hardest thing about being a widow is the fact that it's over. All the intimate love between a man and a woman, the secret looks, the giggles, the sitting close together, the talks, the sex, the joy of just being together is all over. You can't replace the forty-eight years of togetherness. Having had my mom die so early in my life, I learned to enjoy everything to its fullest. But even so, the fun's over. I miss having Patrick as my husband, and I miss being his wife. I have a great support system. I'm grateful for my children and grandchildren, and the friends that God has blessed me with. I would be lost without them. It's been ten months now, and I'm slowly coming to grips with the fact that my old life is over, never to return.

Once Patrick died, my wisdom giver died. There were some life insurance policies, but what to do with them? I paid all of the outstanding bills except for the house balance. There was not enough money to pay it off, but everything else was paid. Some people get lots of insurance money. I got enough, and I believe wasted what was left. When you turn seventy years of age, your insurances are worth one-half of their original value, and the premiums you pay go up. That's good for the insurance companies, but it's not good for your wallet. It's something I didn't know, but I wish I had known.

When the love of your life dies, you get a little foggy. And the people who love you most are loath to inquire about your finances. They inquired, but they didn't want to be pushy; and quite frankly, while I cared about the money, I didn't. I just wanted to be back with Patrick, and for the rest, I was on autopilot. So I wound up after eleven months wondering what I should do.

I knew our savings was running out, but I still had some money. I wonder if it's smart to put away money when you're working without paying taxes on it? It seemed smart, but once you're retired, when you pull that money out, you have to pay taxes on it. The premise was that you'd be making less money in retirement and therefore, be in a lower tax bracket. The truth is that when you receive the money in retirement, it's taxable income, which puts you in the higher money earned and thus, higher tax bracket. If I had to do it again, I would have paid the taxes when I was working and had the money to do so.

I sold the handicapped van hoping someone who needed it would get it. I was going to give it away, but the charity I selected said that all vehicles received would be sold at auction at a wholesale price and that they wouldn't give it to a particular person.

I had a person who wanted to buy the handicapped van, low-ball style. Every now and then, she'd call and inquire about purchasing the van. Before I sold it, I spoke with her husband, and he said they would discuss purchasing the van. I waited one month, and they never called; so in the end, I sold it to Car Max. I figured Car Max would make money on it, but someone who could use it would still be able to afford to buy it. One month after I sold the van, the lady who said she wanted to purchase it inquired about purchasing the van. Too late.

When I sold our handicapped van, they made me put "Deceased" where Patrick's name would go, and then I had to write his name underneath "Deceased." I had to do this for a few times, but it seemed like a million times because my heart cried every time I wrote "Deceased."

I had thought about keeping the van and taking patients to their doctor's appointments, but I'm old and would be hard pressed to help that person if we had a problem. I remember one time Patrick misjudged the ramp and started to fall over the side. A Marine coming out of the restaurant grabbed the power chair and saved Patrick. I thanked him. I thanked him for his service. I tried to give him some money, but he wouldn't take it.

I guess now's the time to say that we have been helped by many people all our lives and that we were grateful. Sometimes, I'd get a flat tire; and while waiting for the Auto Club to come, someone would pull over to the side of the road and offer to help. I've actually had people stop by and change the tire before I got a chance to call the

Auto Club. No, I don't know why I have lots of flat tires. I buy them new and not the cheapest you can buy.

Hundreds of people held the door for Patrick when he was using the walker and was in the power chair. Every now and then, someone would stop by and speak with Patrick when he was in the power chair. He used to be sort of embarrassed by that, but in the same breath, he liked it. Almost everyone looks away from handicappers. They're not sure how to treat the handicapper. The truth is the handicapper would like to be treated like a non-handicapper, but he does appreciate our holding the door for his power chair, or picking up something he'd dropped. I'm not handicapped, but I am four feet, eight and one-half inches tall, and I appreciate when in the grocery store, people would offer to get groceries off the top shelf for me.

A Whole Year

Today was May 18. One year had passed since Patrick passed on. Yesterday, our children, spouses, and grandchildren went to the wall of ashes at the burial ground and looked at Patrick's nameplate. Afterward, we went to dinner at Libations restaurant. After we ate, they went home, and I went to dinner with the in-laws, Patrick's brothers and their wives. No, I didn't eat again; I chitchatted while they ate. Pepper had made dessert; so Brad, Lonnie, and I went to her house after dinner.

We chatted as usual about the past and what it was like for the boys, Patrick, Brad, and Marty, growing up in a military family, the places they'd lived, and the one place with the owl mounted above the fireplace that sort of scared them and in particular, scared Patrick. And about today being one year without Patrick and how long that seemed to me, yet the folks at church said it seemed short to them. And about how their mom was doing in the assisted-living home, moving from the regular side to the dementia side, and the experiences—good and bad—we'd had while visiting her.

The last time, Libby, David, and I visited Patrick's mom, she had been moved to a more intense unit, and we had trouble finding our way. We went outside, through the courtyard, and found an open door. When it was time for us to leave, a lady asked if we would hold the door for her. Of course, we would. It was raining, so she decided to stay in the building. We were really glad she'd decided to stay because on our way out, one of the staff said that the lady was a resident and should not have gone outside.

Marty had taken over Patrick's place in caring for their mother, so they discussed selling her house and things like that. Marty and Pepper's children were there. It was good to see them and to chitchat with them on Sue's budding career and on being a newlywed, and on Tom's recent graduation from college. But that was yesterday, and today was a day for reflection.

This first year, I thought every day of Patrick. I didn't cry every day, but almost every day, I at least teared up. Most of the time, I cried for myself. Self-pity seems crummy, but I believe it was necessary. Lots of times, I'd find myself crying and realize that I was crying grateful tears. God blessed me with Patrick, and with our children and their spouses that we grew to love and got along with, and with our grandchildren. Even so, I miss Patrick.

I gave away Patrick's super-duper motorized power chair and the lift we used to pull him out of bed. The hospital bed, I still have sitting in the den. I gave away most of Patrick's clothes, but I'm always going to keep that green sports jacket that he loved to wear, his pseudo golf jacket. I'll probably sell our house this year. The tax-man said that I would only have two years to sell my home before I would have to pay taxes on any profits made.

I had thought about selling it when Patrick was alive because maintaining it was difficult, but I worried that moving would be terrible for him, so we stayed. The old saying is that a widow or widower should not make any changes the first year, so I stayed in our house.

Roxy and Precious get me up in the morning. I feed them breakfast and open the doggie door, so condos are out because I'm too lazy to harness them up each time they want to go outside. Roxy, being a beagle, likes to lie outside in the grass, so I'd have to be outside with her. A little house with a not-to-big yard would be ideal. Of course, I want a doggie door, one for the house and one for the screened porch.

Regrets

My dad always said that he had lots of regrets. I don't know what they were because I never thought to ask, but when he would say so, I would vow to myself that I wouldn't have any. Well, of course, I have some, but I find that most of my regrets are things that I didn't do, not what I did.

Our friends, Flo and Ryan, had a daughter-in-law who was murdered. I loved that child. I wrote a note for what I wanted to say at her funeral, but I didn't read it because I felt out of place. People from Heather's work spoke, and I was waiting for the rest of her friends to speak, but they didn't. After the funeral, I spoke with some of them, and they hadn't seen her since her wedding. I felt like an idiot. What a terrible person I was to have cheated myself and Heather by not speaking on her behalf.

Perhaps my greatest regret is that, like at Heather's funeral, I sold myself short so many times. I thought that someone could do something better than me, or that I didn't deserve whatever it was. So I didn't do what it was that I could have and should have done. That's dumb. It is a trait that I constantly tried to overcome, but a trait that most of the time overwhelmed me.

I had a patent for a cat leash. Korey was going to invest in it. It was a breakaway collar for the cat's neck, a leash attached to the collar by a hook, and a kneeling pad attached at the end of the leash. You put this on your cat and he/she will stay close to home. I didn't make the cat leash for sale because I was going to install a pond in my backyard, and I realized that if the collar didn't break away, my cat would drown. I just couldn't chance his drowning, so another great idea was down the tubes. Hopefully, another great idea might just pop into my head someday.

There was the time that I found out that the American Girl Doll company had a tea for American Girl Doll parents in New York City. Throughout the years, I had given my three granddaughters American Girl Dolls. I made the reservations for the bus to see the Rockettes, and for the tea. The only problem was that Margot and Savannah were not speaking to each other. I determined that because Savannah was their mother, she would go and that Margot would not go. We went on the trip, but in my stupidity, I had left out the only real doll lover. I should have invited Margot to go too. She and Savannah could have fought it out, and they could have both gone. Sometimes, I'm just plain stupid.

Still Missing Patrick

June 9, 2016, thirteen months after Patrick died, I sit here because I didn't go today to substitute teach and instead, listened to the talk shows on the radio. But I really didn't hear the shows. I just thought about being held by Patrick, trying to recall how that felt, thinking about our talking on and on and analyzing how we did in life. He wondered if we could have done better, but I always told him that I thought we did okay. So I sit here feeling sorry for myself once again, crying, wishing I could him tell him again that I thought we did okay and that I always loved him and I knew he always loved me too.

The other day, I had my taxes done. Holy smokes. Because I hadn't changed my status to single, the government held my taxes based on being married, so I might have to pay a fee because I forgot to withhold enough money. Single people pay quite a higher tax than married people. What a mess.

But I looked over to my right and saw Roxy sleeping on her bed, wagging her tail, having some kind of a fun dream. And to my left, Precious was lying on her back, all stretched out, smiling. That was when I knew everything would be all right.

There are still lots of decisions to be made and lots of changes that will come, but I'm not worried. Even though I miss Patrick (I'm sure I always will), I know that God will give me the wisdom to know what to do and the strength to do it.

The End

About the Author

Mary Ethelyn Wightman was born in St. Augustine, Florida, but spent most of her childhood growing up in Baltimore City, Maryland. As an adult, Mary has lived mainly in Anne Arundel County, Maryland. Her favorite pastime is sitting on her screened porch with her beagle and poodle dogs while reading a book or listening to the radio. She sometimes sings with the radio songs, while her dogs howl along.